Lord Jesus Christ appeared to Two Sisters Year 2013 and 2014 inside the Shrine of the Holy Infant Jesus of Prague

JULIY ISPIRITO

Copyright © 2017 Juliy Ispirito

All rights reserved. No part(s) of this book may be reproduced, distributed or transmitted in any form, or by any means, or stored in a database or retrieval systems without prior expressed written permission of the author of this book.

ISBN: 978-1-5356-0974-6

Table of Contents

Introduction 1

Chapter 1: The Sisters' First Miracle 5

Chapter 2: The Sisters' Second Miracle........................... 15

Chapter 3: Meaning of Green, Brown, and White 40

Chapter 4: Honoring the Almighty Heavenly Mother 43

Chapter 5: My Belief... 49

Chapter 6: Holy Quadrinity and the Holy Grail............... 55

Chapter 7: The Holy Rosary and Miracles 58

Conclusion 71

Picture of the Traveling Infant Jesus
Photo Courtesy of Emma and Rand

Introduction

The Lord Jesus Christ appeared to my baby sister and me two years in a row, in 2013 and 2014, inside the Shrine of the Holy Infant Jesus of Prague. The Lord Jesus Christ appeared to Emma and me unconditionally.

There are several chapels inside the shrine. The chapel that is dearest to my *heart* is the Chapel of the Traveling Infant Jesus. Later, I will tell you why. The other chapels are: the open Chapel of the Holy Infant Jesus of Prague (the small altar has a roof), the small Chapel of Our Lady of Fatima, and the Chapel of the Big Cross. The big cross is mounted at the main entrance. Honestly, I do not know who named the statue *the Traveling Infant Jesus* or why. All I know from my family and friends is that visitors who have visited the Chapel of the Traveling Infant Jesus have seen muddy footprints of a small child heading back toward the grotto of the *Traveling Infant Jesus*. I also heard stories that a little boy appeared to the shrine's visitors asking for food and drink. When the visitors picked up a plate and turned their head back to the little boy to ask what he wanted to eat and drink, the little boy was nowhere to be found.

The Lord Jesus Christ told me to write His messages and to spread His messages to all His people. I have never written a book before. I talked to and asked my Lord Jesus Christ to guide me in writing this book.

I also wrote this book to share the wonderful and amazing experiences Emma and I had inside the Shrine of the Holy Infant Jesus of Prague.

Juliy Inspirito

I am a sinner. My sister is also a sinner. Even though we are sinners, the Lord Jesus Christ chose to appear Emma and me. The Lord Jesus Christ loves all of us unconditionally. Remember this always.

I also want to share with you the way I pray the Holy Rosary and the miracles I experienced every day and every night while praying the Holy Rosary.

I hope that when you finish reading each chapter of this book, you will find comfort, joy, and hope and that your faith and relationship with our Lord Jesus Christ will be at the tightest point in your life.

The Lord Jesus Christ is here on Earth, and the Archangels Michael, Gabriel, and Raphael are with Him. The Archangel Raphael surprised me big time! I will share that surprise with you, too.

Allow me to tell you how my faith and belief in the Traveling Infant Jesus got super strong.

The first time I visited the Shrine of the Holy Infant Jesus of Prague was on July 1, 1986. During this visit, I took my nine-month-old son and his dad with me. On this visit, I witnessed something special. I sat and watched as the "special" event unfolded. My son was riding on his dad's shoulders; he was having a good time. Suddenly, our little boy started kicking and wanted to get down. His dad put him down on top of a well-trimmed lawn. We sat under a tree and watched our son. Our son sat on top of the grass for few seconds, and then he started crawling away from us. He crawled about twelve feet away, and then he stopped and sat on top of the grass and looked up. My nine-month-old son started talking baby talk to "someone." My son clapped his hands while talking to this someone. He giggled and laughed like they were playing peek-a-boo. He reached his arms out while talking to this *someone* and was filled with excitement. I did not see anyone in front of him. The baby talked and giggled for about two minutes.

Lord Jesus Christ appeared to Two Sisters Year 2013 to 2014

Then my son started to crawl farther away from us, as if he were following this someone. I got up and picked him up. My son cried. He looked back, and his little arms tried to reach out to someone; he kicked and cried. I handed him his milk bottle, and then he stopped crying. Again, he crawled away from us, heading toward the same area where I picked him up earlier. He crawled away from us with the milk bottle in his mouth. He sat on the grass, took his milk bottle away from his mouth, and raised it to someone, as if he wanted to give his milk bottle to someone in front of him. He was kicking his little feet while talking baby talk; he was full of excitement.

Whomever my son was talking to was playing with him, my nine-month-old baby boy. They were having so much fun. I realized at that very moment that the Traveling Infant Jesus was playing with my son. It is known that the Traveling Infant Jesus has appeared to so many people in the past.

Then, I noticed my son had crawled toward the Chapel of the Traveling Infant Jesus. From my son's behavior, I knew he was following someone. He continued the baby talk while crawling. My little boy was filled with joy and excitement. I got up and picked up my baby, and we went inside the chapel. I smiled and started conversing with the statue. I asked the Traveling Infant Jesus to guide my son on right path of his life, to be by my son's side always, and to protect him against harm until the end of time. I asked Him to guide me to the right path of life and to protect my family and me always. I offered prayers and many thanks to Him. I promised Him I would return one day and visit. I left the Shrine of the Holy Infant Jesus of Prague filled with joy.

Since that day, my faith, belief, and relationship with the Traveling Infant Jesus has reached its highest point in my life. When I returned to the States, I looked forward to visiting the grotto of the Traveling Infant Jesus.

I have given the Traveling Infant Jesus another name. I asked Him first if it was okay with Him if I call Him the Traveling Niño. During my prayer, I asked the Traveling Infant Jesus if He did not like the name Traveling Niño to please let me know. So far, I have not heard any objection from Him. During my prayers, I address Him as the Traveling Niño.

In this book, I interchangeably address Him as the Traveling Infant Jesus and the Traveling Niño.

The Shrine of the Holy Infant Jesus of Prague is in Davao City, Philippines.

Chapter 1
The Sisters' First Miracle

On Friday, June 28, 2013, my baby sister Emma and I woke up early in the morning and took a taxi to visit the Shrine of the Holy Infant Jesus of Prague. I exited the taxi while Emma paid the taxi driver. I stood quietly outside the gate of the shrine and observed my immediate surroundings. Through the metal fence, I saw the shrine's shrubs and flowers. My heart started to beat faster. I was excited. I noticed that there were no visitors inside the shrine. I heard the birds singing. The shrine was extremely quiet, peaceful, and serene. My sister and I walked toward the front gate and entered. From my July 1986 visit, I recalled seeing the open Chapel of the Holy Infant Jesus of Prague and the Chapel of the Traveling Niño immediately as I entered. Today, I did not see the Chapel of the Traveling Niño. I started to worry but did not say a word to Emma. We walked toward the open Chapel of the Holy Infant Jesus of Prague. When we arrived at the bottom floor of the open chapel, I looked around. The bottom floor, as well as the stairs, was covered with clean and shiny white tiles. At the very top of the white-tiled stairs, I saw the altar of the Holy Infant Jesus of Prague. I took off my shoes and socks. Emma was wearing her slippers. We started walking toward the stairs. Quietly, I told my sister that I did not see the Chapel of the Traveling Niño.

I described to Emma the location of Chapel of the Traveling Niño in relation to the location of the Chapel of the Holy Infant Jesus of Prague. In 1986, as I entered the shrine, the Chapel of the Holy Infant

Jesus of Prague was to my right side, and the Chapel of the Traveling Niño was located straight forward. Emma noticed the sadness and sorrow on my face; it covered my whole being. I was desperate. Lovingly, Emma said, "Maybe they moved the chapel somewhere inside the shrine. Let's climb the stairs and pray to the Holy Infant Jesus of Prague. Let's ask for His help. After we offer our prayers and thanks, we will look for the Chapel of the Traveling Niño."

I told Emma that in 1986 when I visited the shrine, as soon as I entered, I could see the sidewalls of the Chapel of the Traveling Niño. The chapel walls were made of iron or steel. I remembered seeing a small grotto through the gaps of the walls, and the statue of the Traveling Niño was located inside the grotto. To see the statue of the Traveling Niño, I had to go inside His chapel. I asked my sister if she remembered seeing a chapel with the walls and door made of iron or steel. My sister said no. I described to her how small the chapel looked from outside and inside again.

I asked my baby sister another question. "When was the last time you visited the Shrine of the Holy Infant Jesus of Prague?"

Emma responded, "It was 2010." She told me that in the past when she visited the shrine, she went straight to the open Chapel of the Holy Infant Jesus of Prague. Emma said that she stopped by at the shrine on the way home after she finished working. She said that she lit candles, offered her prayers, offered thanks, and went home.

We proceeded to climb the stairs and finally arrived at the altar. I stared lovingly into the eyes of the statue of the Holy Infant Jesus of Prague. I felt this awesome feeling inside of me. The white statue rested inside a man-made hole in a cemented wall. The statue was protected behind a glass door. I continued to stare lovingly at it. The statue was dressed in a long, shiny, glittery, gold "gown." I offered my prayers and my many thanks to Him. I told the Holy Infant Jesus of Prague about my two deployment experiences, the ugliness of the war, the sufferings of the people of the host countries, especially the children, and the endless mortar attacks by the enemies. Then I told the statue that I wanted to visit, talk, and pray to the Traveling Niño, but I could not find His chapel at all. I told the Holy Infant Jesus of Prague that my heart was very sad and that I must find the Chapel of the Traveling Niño and asked Him to please guide me to Him. I had so much to tell Him, too.

As we were about to leave the altar, we saw an older lady cleaning the altar surroundings. I asked her if she could direct us to the location of the Chapel of the Traveling Infant Jesus. I used the words Traveling Infant Jesus so she would understand me. I described to her what the chapel looked like from the outside and inside. The older lady shook her head no. I looked at Emma, and with a low voice, I said, "She works here. She should know where the chapels are located, especially the Chapel of the Traveling Infant Jesus." I became more desperate.

I returned to the altar and looked up at the statue of the Holy Infant Jesus of Prague and told Him, "No one seems to know where the Chapel of the Traveling Infant Jesus is located. No one seems to know where the grotto of the Traveling Infant Jesus is located. It is making me very sad, and my heart aches because I want so much to visit the grotto of the Traveling Infant Jesus. I have so much to tell Him. I have not visited Him for nearly twenty-eight years."

After I talked to the statue of the Holy Infant Jesus of Prague, Emma approached me and comforted me. She told me that we would walk around the shrine and hopefully find the chapel and the grotto of the Traveling Niño. Before I left the altar, I looked at the statue of the Holy Infant Jesus of Prague and offered Him again my thanks for all the gifts and blessings He had blessed me with all my life. I prayed for my baby sister Emma, my other sisters, their husbands and their children, my brother, his wife and their children, cousins, aunts, uncles, relatives, friends, and neighbors. I raised my right hand, waved goodbye, and told Him, "I will visit you again very soon."

We started walking toward the stairs, and slowly we climbed down. Emma comforted me. I was about to cry, but my sister told me not to worry. We arrived at the bottom of the open chapel, and I put my socks and shoes back on and started walking. I saw another chapel to the left of the open Chapel of the Holy Infant Jesus of Prague. The chapel had a roof but no walls at all. This chapel had benches inside. I did not recall seeing this chapel when I visited the shrine on July 1, 1986. We walked toward the wall-less chapel.

As we got closer to this chapel, I noticed a big cross bolted to the front of the chapel. Our Lord Jesus Christ was nailed to this cross. I felt an overwhelming sadness inside of me. We walked slowly toward the cross, and I felt tears rolling down my cheeks.

As I got closer and closer to the big cross, I saw a metal wall nearby the cross. I walked faster. I had found the Chapel of the Traveling Infant Jesus! I made a quick stop at the big cross and offered prayers. I told Emma that I found the Chapel of the Traveling Infant Jesus. I pointed out the chapel to Emma. Hurriedly we walked toward it. The chapel was located in the lower elevation. I could not see the chapel from a distance because another chapel blocked my view; I am vertically challenged.

I climbed down carefully, and my sister followed me. I touched the metal wall with my bare hands. As I walked parallel to the metal walls, I saw through the gaps of the walls a small grotto standing in the middle of the chapel. It looked familiar. I got so excited. With great excitement, I said loudly, "There You are, there You are!" Instantaneously, I saw an apparition of a Little Boy's upper body that came out from the top left of the statue of the Traveling Infant Jesus. The apparition of a Little Boy became more prominent and clearer. The Little Boy turned His head toward Emma and me. I saw His dark brown face and His black hair with big curls. His eyes were wide open and filled with joy. I saw a big smile that lit up his whole face. The Little Boy clapped His hands. He was excited to see us too.

Full of excitement, I kept repeating, "There You are, there You are! I found You! I found You!"

At the same time, Emma said, "Did you see that? Did you see that?"

I said, "Yes."

My baby sister said, "I am seeing a shadow of a Little Boy. I am seeing a figure of a Little Boy come out from the statue of the Traveling Infant Jesus. He is watching and smiling at us. Look at Him! He is watching us. He is smiling at us!"

With a whisper, I told Emma to be quiet. I saw Emma's face full of excitement.

The happy Little Boy watched Emma and me as we walked outside His chapel. As we headed toward the main entrance of His chapel, I turned my head toward the statue and watched the Little Boy watching Emma and me. He was clapping His little hands. I was very happy watching Him, too. The age of the Boy was between eighteen months and two years. The Little Boy's face was full of joy watching Emma and me full of excitement. He looked very healthy and happy. My heart leaped with joy.

As we got closer to the end corner of the chapel wall, before making a left turn heading toward the main entrance of the chapel, the apparition of the Little Boy's upper body retreated slowly back into the statue of the Traveling Niño. With a smiling face, He continued to watch Emma and me as He slowly disappeared into the statue of the Traveling Niño.

The atmosphere inside His chapel was so calm and light. The skin color of the statue of the Traveling Niño was dark brown, as was the skin of the Little Boy. The statue had no covering at all. He was not wearing any attire.

As you see in the picture at the beginning of this book, to His left hand He has a round object that symbolizes the planet Earth. His right hand is raised and making the sign of peace. The tips of the right index and right middle fingers were missing, as if someone had broken the tips of the two fingers intentionally. My sister and I offered chocolate candies, prayers, and a bunch of thanks. The statue was surrounded by fresh flowers. My sister left me standing in front of the statue, and she sat on the bench praying. I talked to the statue of the Traveling Infant Jesus. I told Him that I was looking for Him, but no one seemed to know His location. I told Him, "I was desperate to see You because I have not seen You in almost twenty-eight years. I wanted to talk to You and tell you about my son, my accomplishments, my deployments to Iraq and Afghanistan, my health, and the nurses I worked with."

I told the Traveling Infant Jesus that that I prayed to the Holy Infant Jesus of Prague to guide me to Him. I told Him that Emma comforted me and encouraged me to walk around the shrine hoping to find Him. I said, "I am so blessed and happy that I found You again."

I told the statue of the Traveling Infant Jesus that Emma and I saw an apparition of a Little Boy that came out from His statue and that the Little Boy was smiling at me and Emma. I told the statue that it was Him, the Baby Jesus, who appeared to Emma and me. I offered prayers and said, "Thank You for appearing to Emma and me." I told the Traveling Infant Jesus that I was a sinner and asked Him to forgive me for all the sins I had committed. I told the Traveling Infant Jesus that my sister Emma was a sinner like me, but despite all the sins we committed, the apparition of the Baby Jesus appeared to Emma and me unconditionally. As I told Him that my baby sister and I were sinners, tears rolled down my cheeks. I was choked up while talking to Him. I asked Him, "Kindly forgive me for all of the sins I have committed in this lifetime. Bless, guide, and protect me, my son, siblings, and family until the end of time." I sat quietly next to Emma.

Lord Jesus Christ appeared to Two Sisters Year 2013 to 2014

My baby sister quietly offered her prayers and thanks. We sat on the bench for nearly thirty minutes and meditated. Then Emma started talking to me about the shadow and a figure of a Little Boy that came out from the statue of the Traveling Niño. She said that she saw a Little Boy watching us while we were walking outside the Chapel of the Traveling Infant Jesus. Emma said that the shadow/figure of a Little Boy was smiling at us. Emma also said that the figure watched us for a while before It went back into the statue of the Traveling Niño. I told Emma that I saw It, too.

Emma said, "The Baby Jesus appeared to us. He loves us. He likes us. He blesses us. We received miracles from the Traveling Infant Jesus; the apparition of Baby Jesus appeared to us unconditionally." Emma's face lit up with joy.

My heart filled with joy. We held our hands together and looked at the statue of the Traveling Infant Jesus. I said, "Baby Jesus, thank You very much for appearing to Emma and me. Thank You for loving Emma and me unconditionally."

We left the Chapel of the Traveling Niño and walked slowly toward the Chapel of Our Lady of Fatima. Her chapel was located across from the Chapel of the Traveling Niño. We prayed and offered our thanks. While inside the Chapel of Our Lady of Fatima, I felt some sort of energy pulling me to return inside the Chapel of the Traveling Niño. I told my sister that I must go back inside the chapel, so we went. Suddenly, I felt this wonderful energy, an overwhelming joy as I stepped inside His chapel. I stood up in front of the statue of the Traveling Niño and told Him about my Iraq and Afghanistan deployment experiences, the ugliness of the Iraq and Afghanistan wars, the collateral damages of the wars, and the need to heal my pains and get better. I felt cold air touch my skin and slowly envelope me; it was a truly comforting and soothing feeling. I noticed tears rolling down my cheeks. I stood for a while and then returned to my baby sister, who was sitting on the bench.

My baby sister and I talked about buying souvenirs before leaving the shrine. Emma and I could not remember seeing a souvenir store, but we were sure there was a souvenir store inside the shrine. We just had to find it. Emma and I promised the statue of the Traveling Niño that we would return to talk to Him after we shopped. My sister and I exited the chapel and started walking. Not long after, we found the souvenir store, but it was closed. In the meantime, we went to the restroom. Finally, the souvenir store opened but was not ready. The sales person advised us to wait two minutes. We waited patiently. I told Emma that I planned to buy a statue of the Holy Infant Jesus of Prague and take the statue back with me to the United States. I told Emma I would buy her one, too.

There were so many statues of the Holy Infant Jesus of Prague to choose from. My sister enjoyed looking at every statue on display. My eyes wandered until they landed on three wooden statues of the Holy Infant Jesus of Prague that were separated from the rest. I asked the saleswoman why the three statues of the Holy Infant Jesus of Prague were on the back display cabinet. She said that the statues were defective. Two of the wooden statues' defects were visible; the wood had large cracks. The third statue's defect was not visible. I asked her what was wrong with the third statue. She said that the head of the statue got stuck and could not be removed. She explained to me that the statue's head was supposed to be detachable so it would be easy to put the dress on or take the dress off. Without any reservation at all, I told her that I would buy the third statue. She said she would give me a twenty-percent discount. I told her not to worry about giving me a discount, but she insisted. Emma was holding two statues of the Holy Infant Jesus of Prague in her hands, and she told me that she could not make up her mind which one to buy. She wanted the most beautiful statue, and both were beautiful. I advised her to close her eyes and touch each statue and then listen to her innermost feeling. In less than two minutes, she decided and picked one. I paid for two statues along with other souvenirs. We walked back inside the chapel of the statue of the Traveling Niño.

I stood in front of the Traveling Infant Jesus. I told Him that I bought a statue of the Holy Infant Jesus of Prague and showed it to Him. I told Him that I was going to rub my statue against Him. I proceeded, and then I rested my statue next to him. I made a solemn pact with the statue of the Holy Infant Jesus of Prague and the statue of the Traveling Infant Jesus. I swore, "Starting today, June 28, 2013, until the end of time, you and I are traveling buddies for life. Every time I travel abroad, you are coming with me. We are traveling buddies forever." I held my sister's statue and rubbed her statue against the statue of the Traveling Infant Jesus. I said another prayer: "Kindly protect my baby sister against any harm, and bless her with good health and a long, happy, healthy life." We stayed a little bit longer inside the chapel and meditated. I told the statue of the Traveling Infant Jesus that Emma and I were going back home. I promised that I would be back again. I said thank you once more. Emma did the same. We exited the Chapel of the Traveling Niño. I waved my hands and said goodbye to the statue of Our Lady of Fatima, the statue of our Lord Jesus Christ nailed on a huge cross, and the statue of the Holy Infant Jesus of Prague. We exited the shrine and waited for a taxi to arrive.

Once we arrived home, I told my sister Thea about the apparition of a Little Boy's upper body that came out from the top of the statue of the Traveling Niño. Emma told Thea that she saw the apparition, too. That evening after eating dinner, I told my other sister Liz, aunts, and cousins about the apparition that came out from the top of the statue of the Traveling Infant Jesus and smiled at Emma and me. I explained how he clapped His hands and that He had dark brown skin and black curly hair. My aunts and cousins are devout Roman Catholic. Liz, my aunts, and my cousins told Emma and me that the Traveling Infant Jesus blessed us with a miracle. It is very rare that the Traveling Infant Jesus Christ appears to two sisters on the same occasion.

I flew back to the States, and in September 2014, I visited Davao City again for a house blessing.

Chapter 2
The Sisters' Second Miracle

On Friday September 26, 2014, Emma and I visited the Shrine of the Holy Infant Jesus of Prague together. On this visit, my sister Thea's granddaughter Grasya accompanied us. We arrived at the Shrine of the Holy Infant Jesus of Prague early in the morning. I did not see any other visitors at that moment. My plans were to visit the grotto of the Holy Infant of Jesus of Prague, located at the very top of the hill, first and then visit the Chapel of the Traveling Niño and other chapels inside the shrine.

When we arrived at the bottom floor of the grotto of the Holy Infant Jesus of Prague, Emma decided to stay the behind because Grasya's little feet were in pain. Grasya did not want to walk further, and she was too heavy to be carried. While taking off my shoes, I looked up the staircase and the altar above the stairs. I did not see anyone climbing the stairs. I did not see anyone standing at the top of the stairs. I did not see anyone standing on the altar floor or anyone praying at the altar. I told myself quietly, "I am the first visitor to climb the stairs this morning. This is good. I will have plenty of time to talk to the Holy Infant Jesus of Prague." I walked slowly toward the steps and started climbing with gentle movements. It was a serene and peaceful morning. I was all alone. My left knee started to hurt.

I rested a few seconds and looked up to notice there were only three more steps to the altar floor. At the last step before the altar floor, I looked up again and noticed a young man standing at the edge of the altar floor; he stood right in front of me. Then the young man made gentle strides toward the center of the altar, as if he were floating on air. I was puzzled by the situation. I did not see anyone scaling the stairs at all. I did not see anyone pass by me while I was climbing the stairs. I wondered how this young man got in front of me. The young man stopped walking and stood at the same spot I was planning to stand—at the center of the altar. I wanted to stand at the center of the altar, so I would have a perfect view of the Holy Infant Jesus of Prague while talking and praying to Him. I made it to the altar floor and quietly observed the young man.

I noticed that the young man had dark brown skin and long, thick, shoulder-length black hair with big curls. He wore faded brown cropped pants and a faded forest green chambray shirt. He stood quietly while looking at the statue of the Holy Infant Jesus of Prague inside a man-made hole on the cemented wall and was protected with glass door.

I slowly walked toward him and quietly stood still behind him with questions in my mind. Where did this young man come from? How did he get here without me seeing him? I would have seen him walk in front of me. I would have seen him pass by me. I stood patiently behind the young man and waited for my turn.

In my left hand, I carried the statue of the Holy Infant Jesus of Prague. (It was the statue I bought on June 28, 2013.) The Holy Infant Jesus of Prague was pressed against my breast. I looked up and quietly stared at the statue of the Holy Infant Jesus of Prague and patiently waited for the young man to finish his prayers. After about five seconds, the young man turned left and then walked quietly toward my left side. After he took a few steps, he stopped and turned right. He stood at the right side of the statue of the Holy Infant Jesus of Prague. I stood at the young man's right side. I looked at him and told him, "I am very sorry. I did not mean to interrupt your prayers. I can wait until you are finished with your prayers." He looked at me and slightly nodded his head. I told him, "I will be quick." I saw a tiny smile on his face. I noticed his calm face. I noticed his smooth dark brown skin. I also noticed that his long, black hair was parted in the middle.

The young man looked at me, and then he looked at the statue of the Holy Infant Jesus of Prague that I carried in my left arm. We looked at each other, and I studied his features. He had thick black eyebrows, long beautiful black eyelashes, a long sharp nose, and no facial hair. He looked to be between 5'7" and 5'8", between 170 and 180 pounds, and between fifteen to seventeen years old. He appeared to be of Middle-Eastern descent. He seemed sad, worried, and concerned. Suddenly, his gaze went through me. My mind went blank; it seemed emptied. At the same time, I felt my heart stop beating, and I felt dizzy for about three seconds. It was a different kind of dizziness, but I was very calm and breathed normally. It is difficult to find one right word to describe what I felt at that given moment. The closest thing would be when my papa rescued me. It felt almost like that kind of feeling but better. My heart felt very calm, peaceful, content, and loved. I felt his sadness, his pain, his worries, his suffering, and his unconditional love and kindness toward humans.

Suddenly, I heard him talking to me, but his lips were not moving. I looked into his eyes while he was talking to me. With a soft and sad voice, the young man said, *"I am Thy Lord Jesus Christ. Tell My people I am here."* He stared at me with His loving eyes. I felt a different kind of warmness that I had not felt in my entire lifetime. It is difficult to describe the feeling. His energy penetrated my eyes, my mind, my heart, and my entire being. His gaze went through me. I felt like I was being washed inside out. He continued to gaze at me. I saw the Lord Jesus Christ close His eyes, and when He opened them, He stared at the vast airspace in front of Him. His gaze penetrated through the airspace; it kept on going. I continued to look at Him. His unconditional love changed me. Even now, I can clearly remember the way our Lord Jesus Christ looked.

I stepped forward and stood exactly where my Lord Jesus Christ stood earlier. While I was standing at the right side of my Lord Jesus Christ, I made the sign of the cross on my body. I looked up straight and stared at the statue of the Holy Infant Jesus of Prague. With a whisper, I asked forgiveness for all the sins I had committed, and I offered prayers. I said many thanks for all the blessings with which He blessed me. I asked Him to protect my son, my siblings and their families, my nephews, nieces, cousins, aunties, uncles, and myself. My heart and mind were calmed and filled with love and care. I felt content, peaceful, and filled with joy. While I was standing at His right side, I felt safe, loved, protected, complete, courageous, and inspired. I promised the Holy Infant Jesus of Prague that I would return soon. I turned my head to the left and looked at my Lord Jesus Christ. He stood still while He gazed at the vast airspace. I wanted to come closer to Him so I could kiss His hands and tell Him thank You, but I could not move closer to Him. It was as if I were being stopped by someone. I heard Him tell me, *"Go now, and I will see you again."* I looked at His face and said, "I am done praying here. Thank You for choosing me; You appeared to me unconditionally. I am going to visit the statue of the Traveling Infant Jesus." I saw Him close his eyes and bow His head lightly, and I noticed a tiny smile on His face again. I bowed my head again and turned around and slowly walked down the stairs.

As I walked down the steps, I felt calm, joyful, content, light, peaceful, protected, and loved unconditionally. I felt brand new. I felt like having a new life, a new beginning. It is difficult to describe all the feelings I felt at that very moment. I saw my Lord Jesus Christ's face! We looked at each other, and His gaze penetrated me. It changed me. I feel blessed. I will never forget His gaze. I will never forget His eyes. I will never forget that He smiled at me or that He looked at the statue of the Holy Infant Jesus of Prague I carried and rested on my left breast.

I arrived at the bottom of the steps and walked toward Emma and Grasya. I did not mention anything to Emma about what occurred at the altar of the Holy Infant Jesus of Prague. I put my shoes back on, and slowly we walked toward the Chapel of the Traveling Niño. On the way to the chapel, we stopped at the Chapel of the Big Cross. I meditated for few minutes. I asked forgiveness for all the sins I committed. I offered Him my praise and prayers. I offered Him many thanks for all the blessings He gave me and my family. Emma, Grasya, and I left the Big Cross and proceeded toward the Chapel of the Traveling Niño. The chapel was located next to the Chapel of the Big Cross, but it was on a lower elevation. We watched our steps carefully as we slowly descended to the Chapel of the Traveling Infant Jesus.

Through the gaps of the chapel walls, I noticed there were no visitors inside the Chapel of the Traveling Niño. While we were walking outside the chapel, I felt someone was watching us from inside the chapel, but there was no visitor inside the chapel. Emma said, "It is as if someone is watching us." I did not say a word to her. We walked quietly and entered the chapel. We proceeded straight to the grotto of the statue of the Traveling Niño. Emma, Grasya, and I stood in front of the statue. I made the sign of the cross and said, "Good morning, my Traveling Niño. I am back as I promised you last year. It is so good to see You again." I offered several thanks and prayers.

I heard Emma say, "Good morning, Señor Santo Niño."

Then Grasya started complaining that her feet were hurting again. Emma and Grasya sat on one of the benches inside the chapel. I stood alone in front of the statue of the Traveling Infant Jesus. I told the statue that I brought Him menthol candies, and I hoped He would like them. I placed the menthol candies next to His feet. There were no flowers inside or outside His grotto. I did not see any flowers inside His chapel either; I felt bad about it. I did not bring flowers at all. I promised the Traveling Infant Jesus that next time I visited Him, I would bring Him chocolate candies and flowers. I started talking to the statue of the Traveling Niño. I told Him about my son and his life, my health status, my physical pain, the daily problems at work where a group of nurses verbally and emotionally attacked me on a daily basis, and the ugly memories I had from Iraq and Afghanistan deployments that were still fresh in my eyes, mind, and heart. I asked the Traveling Infant Jesus to bless my siblings and their families with good health, plenty of food to eat, and happy homes. I talked to Him like I talk to my best friends, my siblings, cousins, aunties, and uncles during meal times.

While I was talking to statue of the Traveling Niño, visitors started to arrive. Some visitors stood behind me, other visitors stood on my left and right side, and still other visitors stood in front of me and blocked my view. Quietly, I told the Traveling Infant Jesus that I had so much more to tell Him but did not want other visitors to hear me. I told the statue of the Traveling Infant Jesus, "I am going to leave You for few minutes. I am going to light candles, and I will be back so I can talk to You some more." Excluding Emma, Grasya and me, at least five other visitors were inside the small Chapel of the Traveling Infant Jesus. When I turned around, I saw three more visitors walking toward the chapel door. I made the sign of the cross and left the altar quietly. I told my sister that I was going to light candles, but I would return. I told my sister to hold the statue of the Holy Infant Jesus of Prague for a while.

The candle hut was located outside the Chapel of the Traveling Infant Jesus, just a few steps away. On my way to the candle hut, I saw a few more visitors approach the Chapel of the Traveling Infant Jesus. When I arrived at the candle hut, there was no one inside. I was all alone. I bought about twenty candles. I lit one candle at a time. The first lit candle I offered to the Almighty Heavenly Father. The second lit candle I offered to the Almighty Heavenly Mother. The third lit candle I offered to the Holy Spirit. The fourth lit candle I offered to my Lord Jesus Christ. I lit the fifth candle and offered it to Archangel Michael. The sixth lit candle I offered to Archangel Gabriel. The seventh lit candle I offered to Archangel Raphael. I was about to light another candle when I turned my head and looked inside the chapel. I saw all the visitors inside the chapel were leaving. The visitors' body movements exhibited movements of being rushed by someone to exit the chapel. I was puzzled because the visitors had just arrived.

    The best explanation I can give regarding the visitors' rushed exit from the chapel is that it was as if someone with Divine Power "told" them to leave the chapel at once. I noticed four more visitors outside the Chapel of the Traveling Infant Jesus. They were walking toward the chapel entrance door. The visitors were walking on a small, narrow concrete walkway. Suddenly, the visitors got off the concrete walkway and started walking on top of the grass. I noticed that one man wanted to go inside the chapel, but his body movement made it seem as if "someone" stopped him from entering the chapel and was redirecting him to walk toward the candle hut. The other three visitors with him walked toward the candle hut, too. My sister and Grasya stood next to me. I handed Emma some candles. I looked inside the chapel, and there were no visitors left inside the Chapel of the Traveling Infant Jesus. I lit another candle to offer for my mama who passed away on June 21, 1986. Then I felt a strong energy urging me to look back inside the chapel. I turned my body halfway and looked inside the Chapel of the Traveling Infant Jesus.

    I saw a familiar figure; my Lord Jesus Christ was alone standing inside the Chapel of the Traveling Infant Jesus. My Lord Jesus Christ was standing in front of the statue of the Traveling Infant Jesus. He stood quietly while looking at the statue. My Lord Jesus Christ stood on the same spot where I stood earlier. Honestly, something deep inside of me wanted to go back inside the chapel. I wanted to talk to my Lord Jesus Christ. Then, I got cold feet, and I told myself I better not interrupt His prayer again. I interrupted Him earlier at the altar of the Holy Infant Jesus of Prague because I did not know who He was at that moment. I was about to light my candle when suddenly I felt a strong energy telling me to go back inside the chapel. I told myself quietly, "No, I will not interrupt His prayer again. He is praying. It is not good to interrupt Him." The energy got stronger and stronger.

A presence of stronger energy surrounded me. This energy urged me to walk back inside the chapel. I could not resist the power of this energy at all. I told Emma that I was going back inside the Chapel of the Traveling Infant Jesus. Emma handed the statue of the Holy Infant Jesus of Prague back to me. I handed Emma the remaining candles. Slowly, I walked back toward the chapel holding the statue in my left arm. While walking toward the chapel, I felt different strengths of energies guarding the narrow concrete pathway that led to the chapel's main entrance. At that very moment, it felt like a presence of energies were watching me and protecting me, but my naked eyes could not see anyone. I glanced inside the chapel and saw the back of my Lord Jesus Christ. He stood still in front of the statue of the Traveling Infant Jesus. I did not see anyone else inside the small chapel. The walls of the chapel were made of metal, so it was easy to look through the holes of the walls to see how many people were inside. At that very moment, the only "visitor" I saw inside the chapel was my Lord Jesus Christ facing the statue of the Traveling Infant Jesus.

As I got closer to the chapel's main entrance door, I felt the presence of energy grow stronger and stronger. I was calm. As I arrived at the chapel's main entrance door, I felt two energies. One energy stood at the left side the door, and the second energy stood at the right side of the door. I did not see any person standing on the left side of the door or the right side of the door. I stopped walking. I bowed my head and prayed. The energies were gentle, friendly, joyful, and at the same time very protective. I felt that these energies were beyond this world.

As I stepped inside the chapel, immediately I noticed three more males inside the chapel. I stopped walking and did a quick assessment of them. Two males sat down on the bench next to the chapel's main door. The third male used the bench in front of the two males to kneel on the kneeling board. I was puzzled because the visitors had just arrived. They quietly prayed.

I asked myself, "Where did they come from? I did not see them a few seconds ago. I would have seen them passing in front of me, but I didn't!" I was puzzled!

Of the two males who sat on the first bench, the one who sat next to the aisle had a bigger physique. He was well built and was taller compared to the person who sat next to him. He had straight, black, shiny hair, about an inch long at the top and shorter lengths by the temple areas and the back of the head. The man who sat next to him had longer dark brunette hair, about two inches in length and with light waves. The male who was kneeling in front of them had dirty-blond hair, about two inches all the way around with bigger waves.

I was really puzzled because I had not seen anyone else inside the chapel earlier but my Lord Jesus Christ. I asked myself quietly again, "How did these three people get inside the chapel without me seeing them? I would have seen them passing in front of me!" I walked really slow, and I stopped and stood next to the bench where the two men were sitting down. I turned my body halfway toward them and looked at the two men who sat on the first bench. I stood calmly at the right side of this robust well-built man, his age around late twenties to early thirties. This man's posturing was different from the other male who sat to his left side. This man had a "ready" posture.

From the way he presented himself, he seemed ready to fight anyone to protect his master, his family, or his friends. This man's stature and bearing expressed that he held the highest rank in a group. He looked very healthy and robust. He had a clean-shaved face. He had beautiful deep brown eyes. We looked at each other. His eyes smiled at me. While I stared into his eyes, these questions were inside my mind: *How did you get inside the chapel without me seeing you pass by me? How could I not see any one of you pass by me?* I was puzzled. With a gentle, caring, and soft voice, the man said, "*I am Michael, the Archangel Michael. I am your protector. I am by your side always.*" He smiled at me while telling me these words, but his lips did not move. I was speechless, but my whole being remained calm. My heart leaped with joy. The deepest part of my heart felt an extra joy as if I knew him very well. It is difficult to explain, but that is exactly what I felt. I did not get excited. At that very moment, I felt peaceful, protected, safe, and content. Archangel Michael had light brown skin. He wore a white T-shirt and had on dark navy blue Bermuda shorts. Archangel Michael turned his head to the left, and the man who sat next to him turned his head toward me. This man looked into my eyes. I looked at him curiously.

The man who sat to the left side of Archangel Michael had a lighter brown complexion compared to Archangel Michael. He had a head full of well-managed, light, wavy dark brunette hair about two inches all around. He looked younger than Archangel Michael. I stared into his light brown eyes; he seemed happy. With a smile on his face, he said, "*I am Gabriel, the Archangel Gabriel. I will continue to bring you messages from the Divine Family. I will bring your messages to Them. I am by your side always.*" I did not see Archangel Gabriel's lips move while he talked to me, but I heard his calm, happy, soft voice. He seemed eager and easy to talk with. While staring into Archangel Gabriel's eyes, I found the deepest meaning of faith, patience, understanding, perseverance, love, humility, sacrifice, and kindness. Archangel Gabriel wore a very light-colored brown T-shirt and dark brown Bermuda shorts. Archangel Gabriel turned his head to the front, and he looked at the man who was kneeling in front of them. I looked at Archangel Michael, and I heard his gentle, caring, soft voice tell me to walk forward. I turned right and started walking. While walking, I observed the man who was kneeling.

The man who was kneeling had a light pinkish complexion and a head full of well-managed dirty-blond hair that was about two inches long, curlier than Archangel Gabriel's hair. He looked older than Archangel Michael and Archangel Gabriel. As soon as I passed him, I stopped and turned left. He turned his head toward me and looked into my eyes with a little smile on his face. We stared at each other. With a soft, gentle voice, he said, *"I am Archangel Raphael. I have been by your side helping you taking care of the sick, severely wounded, and emotionally hurt people. I am taking care of you. I am by your side always."* I did not see his lips move either, but I heard his soothing, soft voice. His eyes were between light brown and light orange. I did not see any facial hair. Suddenly, my eyes saw something very surprising. When I looked at Archangel Raphael's chest, I noticed he had bosoms! I could not believe what I saw. I looked at Archangel Raphael's face, head, and chest; Archangel Raphael was a female! From the back, Archangel Raphael looked like a male. I was taught at a very young age that Archangel Raphael was a male. I was taught wrong. Archangel Raphael is a girl. Then I noticed Archangel Raphael wore a sleeveless, light pink dress with a small light pink belt. She smiled at me, and then she turned her head to the center. My eyes got really big, my eyebrows lifted, and my mouth was opened, but no words came out. I heard Archangel Michael's voice telling me to walk forward. Then I heard Archangel Gabriel's voice telling me that the three of them are by my side always. Archangel Gabriel told me to call them whenever I needed help, then he smiled at me again. I will never forget the way Archangel Michael,

Archangel Gabriel, and Archangel Raphael looked. I asked them all to keep the "pictures" of their faces fresh in my memory until the end of time. It appeared that Archangel Gabriel is the youngest of the three. I turned right and started walking forward.

After few steps, I stopped and turned halfway. I looked at each one separately, and they looked at me. I thanked them for appearing to me. I thanked them for protecting me, my airmen, soldiers, sailors, Marines, civilian workers, and patients during the mortar attacks. I thanked them for sending me messages that helped me to solve my problems and for helping me take good care of the severely Wounded Warriors' lives down range and back home. I thanked them for helping me take care of the very sick patients, the emotionally, physically, and mentally hurt patients, as well as the patients' families. I told them that it had been a tough road, but I made it through because they had been there with me along the way. I looked at Archangel Michael, Archangel Gabriel, and Archangel Raphael and bowed my head; they nodded and smiled back at me. I put both of my hands to my lips, gave them a flying kiss, and said thank you once more. I turned halfway and proceeded toward my Lord Jesus Christ.

I felt that Archangel Michael, Archangel Gabriel, and Archangel Raphael appeared to me in human form because the Lord Jesus Christ appeared to me in human form. I believe that the Archangel Michael, Archangel Gabriel, and Archangel Raphael accompanied our Lord Jesus Christ when He appeared to His chosen messengers. I firmly believe that whoever the Lord Jesus Christ chooses to appear to, Archangel Michael, Archangel Gabriel, and Archangel Raphael will also appear to the chosen one. I am a sinner, and yet the Lord Jesus Christ, Archangel Michael, Archangel Gabriel, and Archangel Raphael appeared to me unconditionally.

I walked forward and told myself quietly, "The three archangels are here inside the Chapel of the Traveling Infant Jesus. They are with my Lord Jesus Christ. They are protecting my Lord Jesus Christ, and they are also protecting me." As I quietly uttered these words, I felt lifted. At that very moment, my physical being and my spirit were rejoicing. Miracles were happening right in front of me. My Lord Jesus Christ, Archangel Michael, Archangel Gabriel, and Archangel Raphael blessed me.

I stood quietly behind Him. He looked just as I had seen Him before with the same attire. I noticed the Lord Jesus Christ was wearing a pair of old white tennis shoes and a pair of white socks–not folded at the top. His right hand was holding a small old white washcloth. I noticed the back of His shirt was soaked with sweat. His calves were covered with sweat. I did not notice any hair on His legs, but I noticed His well-defined muscles on His calves. My Lord Jesus Christ has dark brown skin. It is a different shade of brown; it has a tinge of red and orange color mixed together. I have not seen that type of skin color in my life. The tip of His hair touched the bottom part of the collar. I looked at His calves again; big beads of sweat rolled down to His socks. Quietly I told myself, "I wish I had a bottle of water with me; I would give Him the water." About ten seconds later, He faced left and walked smoothly toward my left side, as if He were floating in the air while He walked. He stopped and turned around and faced my direction; He stood less than two feet away from me.

The Lord Jesus Christ stood at the right side of the statue of the Traveling Infant Jesus, and I stood at Lord Jesus Christ's right side. I stepped forward and stood where He had a few seconds ago. I was only about a foot away from Him. Suddenly, I felt this wonderful energy surrounding me. I started talking to the statue of the Traveling Infant Jesus.

I told the Traveling Infant Jesus that I brought my traveling buddy with me—the statue of the Holy Infant Jesus of Prague. I told the Traveling Infant Jesus that I had a little piece of furniture inside my bedroom that I turned into an altar; this was where I placed my statue of the Holy Infant Jesus of Prague. I told Him that I talked to the statue before I went to sleep at night, when I woke up in the morning, and before I went to work early morning. While at work, I also prayed to the Holy Infant Jesus of Prague and the Traveling Infant Jesus. I talked to the Holy Infant Jesus of Prague after I arrived home from work. I continued my conversation with the Traveling Infant Jesus while I stood at the right side of my Lord Jesus Christ. I told the Traveling Infant Jesus that there were seven female nurses I worked with who had given me a difficult time at work. These nurses made up untrue stories against me and accused me of wrong doings, and they harassed, belittled, and intimidated me all day every day. My life at work was extremely painful and difficult. I cried so many times. They spread rumors that I would be fired from work in a matter of days. I was concerned about my military and nursing career. These nurses were planning to harm my military and nursing career that I had worked so hard to earn. These nurses were African American. One Jamaican and the three Caucasian bosses were on their side. Two of the bosses were female, and they made my life horrible. I told the Traveling Infant Jesus that it felt like they were feeding off each other.

One day, the clinic's male boss came into my assigned worked area and asked me when I was going to retire. I was shocked. His behavior toward me was extremely hurtful. I felt harassed by him. I told the Traveling Infant Jesus to protect me against the seven female nurses, the female nurse manager, the female acting nurse manager, and the male clinic boss. I had not done anything that would hurt them. The only thing that I could think of was that I was the only Filipina that worked with them. I always did what was right for the patient. I loved being a nurse. I worked hard to get the job done safely and go home. Maybe they were jealous or perhaps angry because I refused to be part of their group. They felt strong because there were so many of them, and I was the only one.

While I stood at the right side of my Lord Jesus Christ, I uttered each nurse's name and the bosses' names, and I asked the Lord Jesus Christ and the Traveling Infant Jesus to protect me against these people. I offered all these people to the Lord Jesus Christ. Tears rolled down my cheeks while I spoke. Suddenly, I felt energy hug me; the energy enveloped me. I could not stop my eyes from crying. I heard a familiar voice. The Lord Jesus Christ whispered into my ears, *"Do not be afraid. I am with you always."* I felt a big lump inside my throat.

I rubbed the statue of the Holy Infant Jesus of Prague against the statue of the Traveling Infant Jesus. I felt an energy urging me to put my statue on a small piece of furniture located across from my Lord Jesus Christ. The furniture was located to my right side, about three steps away from the center of the grotto of the Traveling Infant Jesus. I walked toward the furniture and placed my statue of the Traveling Infant Jesus on top of the furniture and said, "I am right next to you." I turned around and saw my Lord Jesus Christ looking at me with a smile on His face. We looked at each other. His gaze penetrated me again. His eyes looked happy. I felt my Lord Jesus Christ's energy envelope me. I felt very light, protected, joyful, loved, and complete. I felt wonderful. His smile was very comforting. With a smile on Lord Jesus Christ's face, He looked at my statue of the Holy Infant Jesus of Prague and then stared into the vast space again.

I walked back and returned to where I stood earlier. I started talking to the statue of the Traveling Infant Jesus again. With a low tone of voice and my hands resting on the statue, I told Him about the ugly things I struggled with while in the military. Then I smelled light fragrances of flowers originating from the grotto of the Traveling Infant Jesus, but there were no flowers inside the grotto or around the grotto. There were no flowers inside the chapel. I had not smelled any flowers earlier. I turned my head to the left and looked at my Lord Jesus Christ; He was still staring at the vast airspace. His face looked worried and concerned. The fragrances of flowers increased. I was surrounded by these different fragrances that I had never smelled in my entire life. I loved wearing perfumes, but the fragrances I smelled were far beyond compare. They smelled comforting, therapeutic, and soothing. I felt light. I felt complete—physically, emotionally, and spiritually.

The fragrances engulfed me, cocooned me. I looked at the Traveling Infant Jesus and my Lord Jesus Christ and said, "Thank You very much for these wonderful fragrances of flowers You blessed me with this morning. I have not smelled this kind of fragrance in my whole life. The fragrances that surround me are more blessings from You. Please let these wonderful, amazing fragrances of flowers dwell inside my nostrils and my sinuses forever and ever. Anytime I need to retrieve these wonderful fragrances of flowers inside my nostrils and sinuses, all I have to do is close my eyes, take slow deep breaths while calling Your name silently, and picture the way You look in my mind. Then my Lord Jesus Christ and the wonderful fragrances of flowers will come alive over and over again. I will enjoy these wonderful blessings until the end of time." I offered prayers for my immediate and extended family and neighbors. I prayed for all those people who hurt me at work. I offered every one of them to my Lord Jesus Christ. I prayed for peace throughout the world. I prayed that famine would be eradicated soon. I asked that terrorism and wars would stop. I stood at the right side of my Lord Jesus Christ when I prayed and asked these. I know He heard me.

My sister Emma and Grasya walked in. With a loud voice, Emma said, "Humuta diri Uy! Asa kaha ni gikan!" Which meant, "What smells so good here? Where does this come from?" My baby sister was very surprised about the wonderful smells of flowers. I noticed Emma walked around me and around the grotto and kept on asking, "Where do these fragrances of flowers come from? Smells so good here!" Emma asked me, "Do you smell that, big sister? It smells so good here. I do not know where the smells are coming from." Emma sounded surprised, excited, and at the same time puzzled. Emma was getting quite loud, so I told her to keep quiet. I continued talking to the Traveling Infant Jesus and my Lord Jesus Christ. I told them, "Thank You for the beautiful fragrances You blessed Emma and me with." The various fragrances of flowers became bolder and bolder. I realized at that very moment that the fragrances were coming from the statue of the Traveling Infant Jesus. I smiled, bowed my head, and offered my thanks.

My Lord Jesus Christ moved closer to me. I felt His energy all over me. His energy engulfed me. I felt He hugged me. At the same time, the fragrances of flowers cocooned me. I felt love, His unconditional love. I felt His kindness and protection. As my tears flowed, I said to Him, "I am a sinner, but despite that, You appeared to me. Thank You for loving me unconditionally. I wanted so much to touch and kiss Thy hands, but something always stopped me from doing so. I hope the next time You appear to me, You will allow me to touch and kiss Your hands." My Lord Jesus Christ made a right face and walked slowly toward the chapel door. I wanted to look at Him, but there was an energy stopping me from watching Him leave the grotto of the Traveling Infant Jesus. The wonderful fragrances of flowers continued to surround my sister and me for about forty seconds after my Lord Jesus Christ left. My sister stood at my side and prayed. The fragrances of flowers slowly dissipated and disappeared.

I finished my prayers and made the sign of the cross on my body. I turned around and saw Emma and Grasya sitting on one of the benches closer to me. I looked at the Archangel Michael, Archangel Gabriel, and Archangel Raphael, and they looked at me with smiles on their faces. I smiled back at them. Archangel Michael looked at me with his caring and loving eyes, and then he put his hands together, the right-hand fingers slipped through the left-hand fingers. I sat next to Emma. I told Emma that I was going to visit the Chapel of our Lady of Fatima. I glanced inside the candle hut and saw people leaving the hut and walking toward the chapel. In a matter of two minutes, visitors started to arrive inside the tiny chapel of the Traveling Infant Jesus. I told Emma that I was going to visit the Chapel of Our Lady of Fatima.

The Chapel of Our Lady of Fatima was located across from the Chapel of the Traveling Nino. It would take about two to three minutes to get to the Chapel of Our Lady of Fatima from the Chapel of the Traveling Infant Jesus. Grasya wanted to rest a little bit more. I told Emma that I would wait for them inside the Chapel of Our Lady of Fatima. I handed Emma my statue of the Traveling Infant Jesus; I knelt and made the sign of the cross and exited the chapel.

I walked slowly toward the door. Archangel Raphael was kneeling and looking very focus. Archangel Gabriel looked happy; he was smiling. Archangel Gabriel is a happy archangel. Archangel Michael looked at me. He seemed ready to fight and protect. The three archangels got up and slowly walked behind me. As soon as I exited the Chapel of the Traveling Infant Jesus, I looked behind me but did not see the three archangels; however, I felt a strong energy standing at my left side, right side, and behind me. I walked toward the Chapel of Our Lady of the Fatima and noticed my Lord Jesus Christ standing inside the chapel in the middle of the altar. He was facing the statue of Our Lady of Fatima with His back facing me. I heard a soft voice tell me to kneel on top of the grass, and I kneeled.

As soon as I kneeled on the grass, my Lord Jesus Christ turned left and made His way to the right side of Our Lady of Fatima. He put His hands together in a prayer formation, raised them toward the statue, and then looked at me. I heard the same voice I heard earlier when I was at the altar of the Holy Infant Jesus of Prague. My Lord

Lord Jesus Christ appeared to Two Sisters Year 2013 to 2014

Jesus Christ told me to write and relay His messages to His people. These are my Lord Jesus Christ's messages:

I am the Son of the Almighty Heavenly Father and the Almighty Heavenly Mother. My earthly mother is the Blessed Mother Mary. Men have given Me many names. I am of the same. I am your Savior. I am humankind's only Savior. I am your Lord Jesus Christ. I am here as I promised. The Archangel Michael, Archangel Gabriel, and Archangel Raphael are here with Me. You have seen them with Me today. You will see them again with Me. Tell My people to pray to the Blessed Mother Mary and Me. She is my earthly mother, and I am her Beloved Son. Tell My people that no earthly man can separate the Son of God from His earthly mother. Millions of people knowingly separated themselves from the Blessed Mother Mary. Tell My people that they must pray to the Blessed Mother Mary. Tell My people to pray the Holy Rosary every day.

Tears rolled down my cheeks as I listened to my Lord Jesus Christ's sad voice. I could not stop crying; it was a different cry. I told my Lord Jesus Christ that I would write the messages He told me today and relay His messages to His people. I told my Lord Jesus Christ that I would speak to His people what I witnessed so that people all over the world would know that He is here now and the three archangels are here with Him.

After my Lord Jesus Christ spoke to me, He slowly rested His praying hands on top of the altar, bowed His head, and rested His head on top of His forearms. I watched Him, and I felt His pain and suffering. I bowed my head and said, "I promise I will write the miracles that Emma and I have witnessed here today. I promise I will write Your messages and relay them to Your people. You chose me. I am Your messenger, and I will tell Your people. Thank You, my Lord Jesus Christ. And thank you, archangels, for appearing to me."

At that very moment, I asked my Lord Jesus Christ for forgiveness. I asked forgiveness for all the sins I have committed in this lifetime and forgiveness for all the sins that humankind has committed against the Ten Commandments. I asked the Lord Jesus Christ to bless each human being with a kind heart and mind and a servant's heart, mind, and hands. I asked the Lord Jesus Christ to bless each human mind and heart with kindness and unconditional love, not only for family members and close friends but also for the less fortunate people. I asked the Lord Jesus Christ to bless the world with an everlasting peace.

I asked the Lord Jesus Christ, Our Lady of Fatima, Archangel Michael, Archangel Gabriel, and Archangel Raphael to help me heal every patient I would be taking care of, and their families. Finally, I asked the Lord Jesus Christ and the Archangel Michael to guard and protect me always.

I felt the archangels leave. Emma and Grasya caught up with me and stood quietly next to me. I continued to look at my Lord Jesus Christ. Then I heard His voice tell me, *"Go now and write the messages I have given you today. Do not be afraid. I am with you always."* I bowed my head and said, "I will, my Lord Jesus Christ. Thank You, my Lord Jesus Christ."

I got up. Emma, Grasya, and I walked slowly and rested for few minutes in front of the Chapel of Big Cross. Then we proceeded toward the main entrance of the shrine. Emma started talking to me.

Emma told me that while she was lighting the candles, she glanced inside the Chapel of the Traveling Niño and saw me standing in front of the statue of the Traveling Infant Jesus. Emma told me that she saw a young man standing next to me. Emma said, "You were standing at the young man's right side. I felt something inside of me, like forces of energies, instructed me to return inside the chapel and be with you." Emma told me that she held Grasya's hand and walked slowly toward the chapel. She looked inside the chapel as she walked and noticed that the young man was standing at the altar facing me and her. My sister said, "I saw a smile on the young man's face." She noticed that the young man was staring at the vast airspace. She said, "It was a different kind of stare, as if there were no end." My sister continued telling me what she witnessed. She described the Lord Jesus Christ's appearance, the type of clothes He wore, the color of His clothing, His shoes and socks, the color of His skin, the way His hair was parted in the middle. Emma's description of the Lord Jesus Christ was identical to what I saw. When she got closer to where I stood, she started to smell beautiful fragrances of flowers around me. Emma said, "Humut Kaayo sa nga tanan; pagtuu naku gikan sa imuha ang humut; dili diay. Hahinumdum ako sa sulud sa taxi wala ko kasimhut sa imoha ug pahumut." Which meant, "What smells so good? I thought the beautiful smells of flowers came from you. I said to myself that it cannot be coming from her because I remembered that while we were inside the taxi, I did not smell any fragrances coming from you."

She said that inside the chapel, she came closer to me to smell me, and she found out that the beautiful fragrances of flowers were not coming from me. Emma then thought, *The beautiful fragrances of flowers are not coming from my sister. Where are the fragrances coming from? There are no flowers inside the chapel. I have to check.* Emma continued explaining what she did. "I walked away from you to check where the beautiful fragrances of flowers were coming from, but when I got farther away from the three of you, the beautiful fragrances of flowers did not exist. So I walked back toward the three of you. As soon as I got closer to the three of you—the young man, the grotto of the Traveling Infant Jesus, and you—I started to smell the beautiful fragrances of flowers again. The beautiful fragrances of flowers were concentrated where the young man stood next to the statue of the Traveling Infant Jesus and you. It was like a big circle of fragrance around the three of you. I stopped searching and started praying." Emma's face had a big smile while telling me all of the things that happened. She said, "I will never forget His smile. I will never forget His eyes. I will never forget the way He gazed at the air. His gaze kept on going. It had no end." Emma was filled with joy and amazement; her eyes were glowing.

Outside the shrine, we waited for a taxi to arrive. Emma and I continued to talk. My sister explained to me that the beautiful smells of flowers consisted of fragrances from different types of flowers like roses, camias, ilang-ilang, sampaguitas/jasmin, lilies, and kalatsutsi/plumerias that were all mixed together, but the fragrances she smelled were much better. Emma said, "I have never smelled such beautiful fragrances of flowers in my lifetime; the fragrances I smelled inside the chapel were not from this world." I told her that I had not smelled such beautiful fragrances of flowers in my entire life either. Her description of the young man was exactly as I recalled.

Emma asked me to describe what I saw. I told Emma what I saw. I said that His gaze went through me. It changed me.

I told Emma, "Our Lord Jesus Christ appeared to you and me in 2013 and 2014. Our Lord Jesus Christ chose you and me. You and I are sinners, but our Lord Jesus Christ chose to appear to you and me. Our Lord Jesus Christ chose to bless you and me." Emma and I held hands and embraced. I told Emma that inside the Chapel of the Traveling Infant Jesus, I saw three men. They appeared suddenly inside the chapel. I looked at each one of them, and then they introduced themselves to me. I told her how Archangel Raphael was a woman. Emma said, "I remember seeing two big men sitting down and one big man kneeling, but they looked like foreigners. I did not pay too much attention at them at that moment." I told Emma that our Lord Jesus Christ told me to write what I witnessed today.

We continued to wait for a taxi and then decided to walk down the hill to catch a taxi. While walking, Emma said, "You and I met our Lord Jesus Christ! He looked so far away and so sad and worried."

I told my sister, "I will never forget how His eyes looked at me. I will never forget His gaze. I will never forget that He smiled at me."

Emma said something to me that is still fresh in my mind. "A miracle happened to us again. He appeared to us again. Last year He appeared to us as a little boy, and this year He appeared to us as a young man. He is here; our Lord Jesus Christ is here."

I responded, "Yes, and Archangel Michael, Archangel Gabriel, and Archangel Raphael were with Him. The three archangels are here on Earth now, and they are traveling with our Lord Jesus Christ." I witnessed a puzzled expression on Emma's face! Emma smiled at me.

While I was writing down the story of our miracles, cool air suddenly touched my forehead and forearm, and it enveloped me. It was a comforting, cool air, a different type of coolness. It lingered for about five minutes.

The taxi arrived, and I felt wonderful riding back home. Emma, Grasya, and I arrived home filled with joy and energy. I told my sister Thea, Grasya's grandmother, about what Emma and I saw and smelled inside the Chapel of the Traveling Infant Jesus. Emma told Thea that she smelled beautiful fragrances of flowers near the grotto of the Traveling Infant Jesus, but there were no flowers around. She told Thea where the smell came from—the young man, the grotto of the Traveling Infant Jesus, and me. My sister Thea said, "The Traveling Infant Jesus blessed you and has given you miracles."

I told my religious aunts and cousins about what I witnessed inside the Shrine of the Holy Infant Jesus of Prague and the fragrances of flowers that Emma and I smelled. I told my aunts, sisters, and cousins that the Lord Jesus Christ appeared to me first, and I described His appearance. One of my cousins asked, "Dark brown skin?" I was not surprised at her question. We grew up seeing statues of the Lord Jesus Christ with white skin. We grew up seeing white-colored statues of our Lord Jesus Christ, the Blessed Virgin Mary, archangels, and saints. I immediately thought that the Lord

Jesus Christ, the Blessed Virgin Mary, archangels, and saints are Caucasians. I was not surprised when my cousin was surprised. I was surprised, too. From what I saw, I believe that the Lord Jesus Christ inherited His skin color from the Almighty Heavenly Father, the Almighty Heavenly Mother, and His earthly mother—the Blessed Virgin Mary.

I told my family that they must pray to the Blessed Mother Mary. They must pray the Holy Rosary every day. I informed my family to forgive those who hurt them and ask forgiveness from those whom they hurt. I advised my family to share food, water, clothes, and money with those who are truly in need; to dedicate time to visit sick and poor neighborhoods; to volunteer time helping people who need shelter; not to be selfish, greedy, and hateful because this is not the way to our Lord Jesus Christ's kingdom; not to abuse the kindness of family; to open hearts and minds to the poor people, the sick people; to give unconditionally to the poor and sick. I told them, "You learned forgiveness, kindness and love from your church services. Once you are outside the church, you must execute what you learned from your church services. Do not leave them inside your church. If you want to see our Lord Jesus Christ, follow what He did. The Lord Jesus Christ never chose who He helped, cured, and fed. That is what unconditional love and kindness is all about."

I told my family about the three archangels and how they introduced themselves to me one at a time in human form, with Raphael being a woman. They were shocked into silence.

I advised my family members and neighbors to pray to our Lord Jesus Christ and the Blessed Mother Mary day and night; to pray the Holy Rosary every day; to repent and to return to Lord Jesus Christ; and to accept our Lord Jesus Christ wholeheartedly and believe in His words and His works. I informed my family about my new belief; I believe in the Holy "Quadrinity": the Almighty Heavenly Father, the Almighty Heavenly Mother, the Lord Jesus Christ, and the Holy

Spirit. They got so quiet. I explained to my family that the Blessed Virgin Mary is our Lord Jesus Christ's *earthly* mother. Our Lord Jesus Christ has a Heavenly Mother and I call her *the Almighty Heavenly Mother*.

I flew back to the States and returned to work.

Chapter 3
Meaning of Green, Brown, and White

One morning while making coffee, I turned my radio on. I heard the radio announcer talk about the effects of deforestation and global warming. To me, deforestation means the permanent harmful destruction of the forest through cutting down trees to make spaces available for farming, such as livestock, grains, vegetables, coffee, and/or building new housing or businesses.

With this in my mind, I remember the faded green chambray shirt and the faded brown crop pants that our Lord Jesus Christ was wearing when He appeared to Emma and me.

I believe that green represents life. Brown represents the soil of the earth, and white means purity and cleanliness. The small wash cloth represents a flag. I have another meaning for the color white: to surrender negative behaviors in order to start a cleaner life.

My own interpretation of the faded green shirt is that it represents deforestation. Numbers of trees have been cut down from forests worldwide; the former forests have been converted into commercial lands. I learned from my elementary science teacher that the leaves of trees process oxygen that is vital to human existence. I believe that the leaves of the trees have helped in controlling the earth's temperatures. One negative effect of deforestation is the rising of earth's temperature, also known as global warming. Another negative effect of warmer temperatures is the melting of the ice in the Arctic region of the earth, which has caused the sea levels to rise.

One day I went to a local restaurant and ordered baked fish for dinner. While waiting for my order, I heard two people behind me talk about the melting ice in the Arctic region. The two men talked about the effects of global warming and the future of world.

I strongly believe that the sea level is rising because when I visited my hometown in 2013, I noticed that the sea was getting closer to my parents' old home. Several houses that were built nearby the seashore are now getting closer to our home. I believe that as the ice continues to melt, the sea level rises, and as the sea level rises, it claims lands. Lands on earth will slowly fade and disappear; these lands will rest under the ocean.

With this proof, the faded brown cropped pants that our Lord Jesus Christ wore when He appeared to me represent the fading lands on earth that are slowly claimed by the rising sea level. If humans do not stop these destructive behaviors, we are bound to lose our only home in this galaxy.

Now, it makes sense to me why our Lord Jesus Christ was wearing plain old white socks and a pair of old white shoes. My own interpretation of the socks and shoes is "protection." To me, this is significant. We humans must unite to protect the remaining trees in the forests. I strongly believe that the trees help sustain the earth's temperature. All of us have only one home, Earth. We must protect our only home. The white shoes and socks mean that we must reuse old items via recycling. Through recycling, we can save one tree at a time. We can save one forest at a time. We must protect planet Earth from further destruction.

July Inspirito

Our Lord Jesus Christ was holding a small, old, white washcloth in his right hand. My own interpretation of the washcloth is that it represents the flag of surrender, or giving up. We can give up two to four hours a week to take care of our planet Earth, one small step at a time. Let us clean up our own negative thoughts, actions, and behaviors one small step at a time.

Chapter 4
Honoring the Almighty Heavenly Mother

This chapter is wholeheartedly dedicated to the Almighty Heavenly Mother. First, I am going to tell you a short story about my religious background.

I grew up in a Catholic family. From primary to elementary school, the Catholic religion class was part of the school's curriculum. I was taught at a very young age about the Holy Bible. During my high school life, my parents sent me to a private Catholic school that was managed by the Sisters of the Presentation of Mary. My religion teachers were Sisters (nuns).

One time, the religion teacher assigned each student to read and study the Old Testament. I was assigned to read and study the book of Exodus from chapters 1 to 25. I had to write my own interpretation and understanding about those chapters. In addition, I had to stand up in front of the class and share with them what I learned from those chapters. I was about fourteen years old. Then the Sister asked questions, and I had to provide some compelling answers. I learned from other students' reports on the Old Testament. My religion class also taught me that God told Abraham that his wife, Sarah, would be pregnant and instructed him to name their son Isaac. My class also taught me that man and woman were created according to God's own image and likeness. This is my own interpretation of the words "own image and likeness." I am going to clarify the word *likeness* according to my own interpretation.

When a man likes a woman, and the woman likes the man, courtship happens. Both fall in love with each other, and then they get married. Through the sacrament of Holy Matrimony, man and woman become husband and wife. The husband and wife become **one unit**. In the old-fashioned way, the wife takes the husband's last name. For example, if the husband's last name is Rose, and they get invited to a wedding ceremony, the invitation card will be addressed to Mr. and Mrs. Rose. The two individuals become one unit. The concept of liking another individual and becoming a single unit was inherited from our Divine Creator's heavenly lifestyle. Humankind inherited the marriage idea from our Divine Creator, the Almighty Heavenly Father, and the Almighty Heavenly Mother. Humankind was created according to God's own likeness. Therefore, I am going to state that the Almighty Heavenly Father has a wife. I named His wife the Almighty Heavenly Mother.

Going back to my high school life, I learned from my religion class that man and woman were created according to God's own image. My own interpretation of this is that man inherited the Almighty Heavenly Father's inside and outside features. Woman inherited the Almighty Heavenly Mother's inside and outside features. The special feature of a healthy woman is the ability to carry a fetus inside her womb and give birth to a child. Other women are blessed to carry two or three fetuses inside their wombs in one conception. The ability of a healthy woman to carry a fetus and give birth to a child separates her from man. Therefore, the Almighty Heavenly Father has a wife, the Almighty Heavenly Mother, and They have a son, the Lord Jesus Christ.

I have changed my belief and started praying to and praising the Almighty Heavenly Mother because She deserves my love, respect, devotion, and praise. The Almighty Heavenly Mother has been deleted from the Holy Bible and from our teaching. I believe that only powerful men from the past centuries had the abilities to delete Her name. I have a feeling that powerful men in the past centuries were "afraid" of Her divine power. The only way for these men to overcome the feeling of fear was to delete this Divine Woman from the Holy Book. They deleted Her name from the Holy Bible and other Holy Books and in order to stop the believers and followers praising and praying to Her. This is the very reason why the Almighty Heavenly Mother has not been mentioned in the Holy Bible and does not appear in any of the prayers that were taught to me.

I learned from my high school religion classes that after the resurrection of our Lord Jesus Christ, the names of the Blessed Mother Mary and Mary Magdalene were rarely mentioned in the Holy Bible. Was it the will of a powerful earthly man who ordered someone to erase the name of the two powerful women from history? That's something to think about.

I am not asking you to believe me; I am only sharing what I believe. Think about how humankind was created according to God's own image and likeness. Let's say, you are a healthy single man and meet the girl of your dreams. You like her very much, and she like you, too. Both of you fall in love with each other. You get married, and she gets pregnant and has your babies.

Prior to September 2014, I prayed every day, but I did not pray the Holy Rosary on a daily basis. And then I experienced difficulties and hardships at work. I mentioned them to you in Chapter 2. Since then, I pray the Holy Rosary on daily basis. I listened to my Lord Jesus Christ's message. He protected me. Archangel Michael, Archangel Gabriel, and Archangel Raphael protected me. They fulfilled their promises to me.

Around May 2015, I spent my one-hour lunch break praying the Holy Rosary inside Saint Joseph Catholic Church or inside Saint Patrick's Chapel. Around December 2015 inside Saint Joseph Catholic Church, I kneeled, closed my eyes, and started praying the Holy Rosary. Suddenly, a breeze of cool air hugged me. I heard a soft, male voice tell me, "Pray to the Almighty Heavenly Mother, and pray to the Blessed Mother Mary." I was puzzled by the message.

I asked the Almighty Heavenly Father, the Lord Jesus Christ, and the Holy Spirit to help me understand the message. That night, inside my bedroom while I was praying, a cool breeze hugged me. It was a different kind of coolness; the energy hugged me for about three minutes. It is difficult to describe. Then I remembered Lord Jesus Christ message when He appeared to me on September 26, 2014. The Blessed Virgin Mary is the Lord Jesus Christ's earthly mother. The Almighty Heavenly Mother is the Lord Jesus Christ's heavenly mother. I realized I was too slow writing His Message. I had to dedicate time to write down Lord Jesus Christ message to His people, to pray to His Almighty Heavenly Mother. To pray to His earthly mother, the Blessed Mother Mary.

The same night, I had a deep conversation with the Almighty Heavenly Father and the Lord Jesus Christ. I told Them that I was going to include the Almighty Heavenly Mother in my prayers. I told them I made a few changes with known prayers. I include the Almighty Heavenly Mother when I make the sign of the cross; when I say the "Glory Be to the Father" Prayer; when I say the Lord's Prayer; and when I say the Apostles' Creed Prayer. I told Them that I added the Almighty Heavenly Mother in the prayers. She deserves to be honored, praised, loved, and talked to. I asked both of Them to stop me from writing this chapter if I was wrong to include the Almighty Heavenly Mother in the prayers, "If you do not want me to include Her in the prayers, please let me know." I have not heard anything from Them at all. Instead, my life is getting better. When minor or major challenges in life happen, I pray to my Lord Jesus Christ, Archangel Michael, Archangel Gabriel, Archangel Raphael, and they continue to bless me.

Making the Sign of the Cross
With the tips of my right-hand fingers, I touch my forehead and utter, "In the name of the Almighty Heavenly Father." With the same fingers, I touch the center part of my chest and I utter, "And of the Almighty Heavenly Mother." With the same fingers, I touch my left shoulder and utter, "And of the son my Lord Jesus Christ." With the same fingers, I touch my right shoulder and utter, "And of the Holy Spirit. Amen."

This Is How I Pray the Apostle's Creed Prayer
I believe in God, the Father and Mother Almighty, Creator of heaven and earth. I believe in the Lord Jesus Christ, the only Son of God, Who was conceived by the power of the Holy Spirit, was born of the Blessed Virgin Mary, suffered under Pontius Pilate, was crucified, died, and was buried. He descended into hell. On the third day, He rose again from the dead. He ascended into heaven and is seated at the right hand of God the Father and Mother Almighty. From there He will come again to judge the living and the dead. I believe in the Holy Spirit, the Holy Catholic Church, the communion of saints, the forgiveness of sins, the resurrection of the body, and life everlasting. Amen.

This Is How I Pray the Lord's Prayer
Our Almighty Heavenly Father, our Almighty Heavenly Mother, who art in heaven, hallowed be Thy names. Thy kingdom come, Thy will be done, on Earth as it is in heaven. Give us this day

our daily bread, and forgive us our trespasses, as we forgive those who trespass against us. Lead us not into temptation but deliver us from evil. Amen.

This Is How I Pray the Hail Mary Prayer
Hail Mary, full of graces, the Lords are with Thee. Blessed art You among women and blessed is the fruit of Your womb, Lord Jesus Christ. Holy Mary, Mother of God, pray for us sinners now and at the hour of our death. Amen

This Is How I Pray the "Glory Be to the Father" Prayer
"Glory be to the Almighty Heavenly Father" (with the tip of my right-hand fingers, I touch my forehead) "and to the Almighty Heavenly Mother" (I touch the center of my chest) "and to the Son my Lord Jesus Christ" (I touch my left shoulder) "and to the Holy Spirit" (I touch my right shoulder) "as it was in the beginning, is now, and ever shall be world without end. Amen."

I found calmness, peacefulness, and constant heavenly support while writing this chapter. There has been a presence of cold air that has constantly visited me while writing this book. It felt like I was being guarded and protected. It is difficult for me to explain every "miracle" that happened to me while writing this book.

Since I included the Almighty Heavenly Mother on the known prayers, I have encountered so many miracles, and miracles continue to happen to me up to the present time. My life is full of joy.

Chapter 5
My Belief

I believe that the cataclysmic Flood that cleansed the earth devastated the Almighty Heavenly Father, the Almighty Heavenly Mother, and our Lord Jesus Christ. They love humankind very much. I believe that the Almighty Heavenly Mother and the Almighty Heavenly Father had a long conversation after the Flood. They planned to repopulate the earth.

The Almighty Heavenly Father and the Almighty Heavenly Mother's unconditional love toward humankind was endless. To save humankind, They came up with another plan: to give humans written guidance. They sat and created the Ten Commandments of God. The Ten Commandments are easy to read, understand, and follow because humans were created according to God's own image and likeness. Humans were blessed with wisdom, intelligence, understanding, hearts, minds, and much more.

Back when I was in high school, I learned from my religion class that God gave Moses the Ten Commandments. These commandments were the written instructions that were inscribed in stones for humankind to obey. We failed to obey the Ten Commandments of God. God's people continued to commit the Seven Deadly Sins over and over again. People continued to disobey the Ten Commandments and failed to ask the Almighty Heavenly Father and the Almighty Heavenly Mother for forgiveness

People continued in their disobedience, and violations of the Ten Commandments raised red flags in heaven. The people's disobedience caused deep sadness and growing concerns in heaven. The Almighty Heavenly Father and the Almighty Heavenly Mother continued to talk. They finally came to a sad decision.

They decided to cleanse the planet Earth again—another catastrophic event. The earth was cleansed by flooding. I believe they planned for a slow, agonizing punishment. The earth would experience years of drought—forty years of continuous drought. All living things that depended on water for existence would perish slowly. Jesus Christ heard His Parents' sad decision, and it worried Him. Our Lord Christ Jesus Christ watched people closely, and He learned to love humankind unconditionally. As His Parents made plans on when to start the cleansing process, Lord Jesus Christ approached His Parents. With a loving and caring voice, He asked His Heavenly Parents not to rush with their catastrophic plan. Lord Jesus Christ convinced His Heavenly Parents that He would help educate man according to the Ten Commandments They sent. He presented His plan of action to His Parents. While He spoke about His plans, the Almighty Heavenly Mother cried and said, "No!" She looked at the Almighty Heavenly Father with tears in Her eyes and rolling down Her cheeks. She told the Almighty Heavenly Father to say no to Their Son's plans. Lord Jesus Christ persuaded His Parents and begged them to give humankind one more chance to redeem themselves. He rationalized with His Parents. He explained to His Parents that He observed that there were so many good, kind, and loving people on Earth.

He said, "These good people will become My disciples, preachers, and messengers. People who continue to disobey Me will not be saved by Me. People who will not believe in Me will never be able to see Our Kingdom in heaven. I will go to Earth and save as many as I can, and those I save will save one person at a time in My name. I will give My life to save humankind because I love them unconditionally." Lord Jesus Christ assured His Heavenly Parents that He would return to Them once He completed His earthly mission. He promised His Heavenly Parents that He would return to Earth one more time. Lord Jesus Christ said, "The second time I return to Earth, I will not suffer and die on the cross for humankind. I have done that already. I will return to Earth to choose the right person to help Me save humankind. Each person to whom I choose to appear will know it is Me. Once that person stares into My eyes, he or she will recognize it is Me. I will speak to that person and tell him or her that I am Jesus Christ the Son of God. He or she will be standing, sitting, kneeling, or lying down on My right side. The people to whom I choose to appear will see Archangel Michael, Archangel Gabriel, and Archangel Raphael with Me. There will be many clues that will help the person to recognize that it is Me. I will appear to any person who has a kind and loving heart and mind. I will appear to any person who believes in doing the right thing because they believe in the Almighty Heavenly Father, the Almighty Heavenly Mother, and Me. Humankind must follow My examples, so they can be saved by Me. I cannot save people who continue to commit the deadly sins; I must let go of them. The second time I return to Earth, I will save as many people as I can in Thy names. This is My solid promise to You, My loving Parents."

    The Lord Jesus Christ emphasized to His Heavenly Parents that all the capabilities He needed to accomplish His earthly mission were available: the archangels, the guardian angels, and the Holy Spirit. He said, "With all of them by My side, We can save humankind." Lord Jesus Christ lovingly told His Parents that He loved humankind unconditionally, even though people kept on committing sins. He knew that humans needed to be taught, and they needed a loving and caring Teacher. Lord Jesus Christ offered Himself to teach people. His Parents did not like His idea, but the Lord Jesus Christ continued to persuade them. The Almighty Heavenly Mother continued to cry. The Almighty Heavenly Father remained quiet. Lord Jesus Christ promised Them He would return to Them after His mission was completed.

It is my belief that the Almighty Heavenly Father and the Almighty Heavenly Mother called an emergency meeting. They summoned the Holy Spirit, Archangel Michael, Archangel Gabriel, Archangel Raphael, and their only beloved Son, the Lord Jesus Christ. The Almighty Heavenly Father and the Almighty Heavenly Mother informed Them about the problems—us, the sinners. They planned to cleanse the earth like They had done thousands of years ago in the cataclysmic Flood and to start repopulating the earth after the cleansing. The Heavenly Father told His audience that Their beloved Son asked Them to give humankind one more chance to save themselves. He told His audience that the Lord Jesus Christ offered Himself to go down to Earth to save humankind. The Almighty Heavenly Mother continued crying. Lord Jesus Christ held Her hands and told Her, "Mother, I promise; I will be back after I complete my earthly mission."

After an agonizing discussion, the Almighty Heavenly Father and Almighty Heavenly Mother agreed to their Son's painful and sad solution, sending Jesus to Earth to save humankind. The Almighty Heavenly Father consoled His wife quietly. They talked and came up with a plan.

The Almighty Heavenly Father and the Almighty Heavenly Mother informed Their audience that They must find a virgin woman to carry the Lord Jesus Christ inside her womb. It got very quiet. Then the Almighty Heavenly Father told His wife, "The archangels must go down to Earth and find a virgin woman to carry the Holy Infant Jesus Christ inside her womb."

Before the Almighty Heavenly Father could talk more, in unison the three archangels uttered loudly the name Mary, pointed to Earth, and said, "We know where Mary lives." The Almighty Heavenly Mother remained quiet while studying the Virgin Mary. Then She whispered to the Almighty Heavenly Father and said that the Virgin Mary had all the good qualities She looked for to carry Her beloved Son. They told Their audience that the Virgin Mary would carry the Lord Jesus Christ inside her womb. The Almighty Heavenly Father and Almighty Heavenly Mother asked their audience who would volunteer to go down to Earth and inform the Virgin Mary about this special mission. In unison, the Holy Spirit, Archangel Michael, Archangel Raphael, and the Archangel Gabriel raised their hands and said, "I'll go." They chose Archangel Gabriel.

Archangel Gabriel visited Virgin Mary and informed her that inside her womb she would be carrying the Son of God. The Holy Spirit was tasked with a special mission. As mentioned in the Apostle's Creed Prayer, the Baby Jesus Christ was conceived by the power of the Holy Spirit.

The Almighty Heavenly Mother was extremely protective of Her beloved Son, Jesus Christ. She called the Holy Spirit, Archangel Michael, Archangel Gabriel, and Archangel Raphael and told them to protect Him and Mary. The Almighty Heavenly Mother repeated Herself and ordered the Holy Spirit and the three archangels that they must monitor the execution of the plan closely, to protect Virgin Mary and the baby Jesus Christ at all times. They said, "We will."

The Blessed Virgin Mary delivered our Lord Jesus Christ inside a stable. The Lord Jesus Christ preached His Heavenly Parents' message and offered services to poor people. Our Lord Jesus Christ was betrayed by one of His disciples. Our Lord Jesus Christ was condemned to die on the cross, and He suffered. He was flogged, whipped, crowned with thorns; he carried the cross, stumbled to the ground three times while carrying the heavy cross on His shoulder, and at the same time was whipped. Our Lord Jesus Christ was nailed on the cross; He suffered too much. He died on the cross to save humankind. His enemies were not done; a spear was pierced into His lifeless body to ensure our Lord Jesus Christ was dead. Our Lord

Jesus Christ endured the pain, suffering, starvation, and thirst to save us, the sinners. He gave up His life to save humankind.

The Almighty Heavenly Father and the Almighty Heavenly Mother suffered heartache and sorrow watching Their beloved Son condemned to die on the cross. Their beloved Son was crucified on the cross to save you and me, to save us all—the sinners.

Chapter 6
Holy Quadrinity and the Holy Grail

I believed in the Holy Trinity. As I grew older and got educated, I started to believe that my Lord Jesus Christ has a heavenly Mother. I started believing the heavenly power of the Almighty Heavenly Mother and established a solid relationship with Her. I now believe in the Holy Quadrinity.

The Holy Quadrinity includes God the Almighty Heavenly Father, God the Almighty Heavenly Mother, God the Son Lord Jesus Christ, the Holy Spirit. I believe that the four of Them truly represent the four cardinal points of our planet Earth: north, south, east, west. I also believe that the four of Them represent the four end-points of the Holy Cross where our Lord Jesus Christ was nailed and died to save us. With the tip of a pencil, I started connecting each end point of the cross, and the result was a shape of a circle but not a perfect circle. My interpretation of this shape is that it represents the people who live on the planet Earth. Earth is our home. If all of us follow the teachings and works of our Lord Jesus Christ, all of us will be saved. We can save the earth as well. We must unite and save the planet Earth from further destruction. We must render kindness and unconditional love to the less fortunate people and those who cannot protect and provide for themselves. The rich men and women can provide on-the-job training, vocational education, and job opportunity to the able individuals. These are the ways to the Lord Jesus Christ. He will appear to you unconditionally. The Archangel

Michael, Archangel Gabriel and Archangel Raphael will appear to you, too. It happened to me and my sister Emma.

I also believe that the deepest meaning of the forty days that are mentioned in the Holy Bible represent the four Divine Persons in the Holy Quadrinity. The number zero that appeared after the number four represents the planet Earth where humans live. For whatever reason, powerful earthly men in the past discredited, disrespected, dishonored, and slowly erased the Almighty Heavenly Mother from the rest. I believe that these powerful earthly men created the belief of the Holy Trinity: the Almighty Heavenly Father, the Son Lord Jesus Christ, and the Holy Spirit. It is very sad. Currently, some denominations have removed the Blessed Mother Mary in their practice and teachings. Two powerful women in Jesus's life do not receive full acknowledgment, praise, love, respect, or devotion.

Many men and women continue to seek the Holy Grail. I feel that men and women who seek the Holy Grail seek a solid item. I strongly believe that the Holy Grail is not a tangible item but that it is composed of two Divine Beings. I believe that my Lord Jesus Christ and the Blessed Mother Mary represent the Holy Grail. The day the Lord Jesus Christ appeared to me inside the Shrine of the Holy Infant Jesus of Prague in Davao City, I noticed something special. While I was kneeling on the grass and watching the Lord Jesus Christ standing at the right side of the statue of the Our Lady of Fatima—another nickname of the Blessed Mother Mary, I noticed a shape. When our Lord Jesus Christ put His hands together, the shape formed into praying hands. He rested His praying hands on top of the altar of Our Lady of Fatima. Then He rested His head on top of His forearms. That specific body alignment and the placement of the statue of Our Lady of Fatima created a shape, a shape of a chalice. The Lord Jesus Christ is the body and the base of a chalice, while the Blessed Mother Mary represents the cup. For me, the Holy Grail is the Blessed Mother Mary and the Lord Jesus Christ. When I pray the Holy Rosary, I continue to offer prayers to my Holy Grail. I live a happier life. I surrender any type of stressors that come my way to my Holy Grail—the Blessed Mother Mary and the Lord Jesus Christ. They visit me every time I pray the Holy Rosary. It is an awesome feeling.

From 2013 to 2015, I experienced hardships and difficulties at work. I prayed to my Lord Jesus Christ and to the three archangels. I also prayed to my Holy Grail. I also asked Archangel Michael, Archangel Gabriel, and Archangel Raphael to protect me from negative people at work, and my prayers were answered. I thanked Them for saving me.

Since I was a young girl, I have heard many stories about the Holy Grail. I heard that the Holy Grail is a chalice. I heard stories about the healing power of the Holy Grail, that whoever finds the Holy Grail will never die. The Holy Grail gives everlasting wealth and power. Unfortunately, no human being has found the Holy Grail. Humans have been looking for this one tangible item. It makes sense to me now that the Lord Jesus Christ has told me His message: "Tell My people to pray to the Blessed Mother Mary and Me. She is My earthly mother, and I am Her beloved Son. Tell My people that no earthly man can separate the Son of God from His earthly mother."

Therefore, every time a person prays the Hail Mary Prayer, the Blessed Mother Mary saves that person's prayers inside Her heart. When difficult times come, that person must pray to the Blessed Mother Mary for help. The Blessed Mother Mary will send Her blessings.

I found my Holy Grail when I was not looking for it. The Lord Jesus Christ helped me to find it.

Chapter 7
The Holy Rosary and Miracles

I learned to pray the Holy Rosary when I was in high school. My parents sent me to a private Catholic school. As I moved on with my life, my friends and acquaintances invited me to attend Holy Rosary Prayers in their homes. I participated praying the Holy Rosary Prayers inside churches or chapels. Even though my life got busy, I have not forgotten the Joyful Mysteries, the Sorrowful Mysteries, the Glorious Mysteries, and the Luminous Mysteries.

I mentioned in Chapter 4 my new way of saying the following prayers: the Apostles' Creed Prayer, the Lord's Prayer, the Hail Mary Prayers, and the "Glory Be to the Father" Prayer. This is how I pray the Holy Rosary.

Making the Sign of the Cross
With the tips of my right-hand fingers, I touch my forehead and utter, "In the name of the Almighty Heavenly Father." With the same fingers, I touch the center part of my chest, and I utter, "And of the Almighty Heavenly Mother." With the same fingers, I touch my left shoulder and utter, "And of the son my Lord Jesus Christ." With the same fingers, I touch my right shoulder and utter, "And of the Holy Spirit Amen."

The Apostles' Creed Prayer
I believe in God, the Father, and Mother Almighty, Creator of heaven and Earth. I believe in the Lord Jesus Christ, the

only Son of God, Who was conceived by the power of the Holy Spirit, was born of the Blessed Virgin Mary, suffered under Pontius Pilate, was crucified, died, and was buried. He descended into hell. On the third day, He rose again from the dead. He ascended into heaven and is seated at the right hand of God the Father and Mother Almighty. From there He will come again to judge the living and the dead. I believe in the Holy Spirit, the Holy Catholic Church, the communion of saints, the forgiveness of sins, the resurrection of the body, and life everlasting. Amen.

The Lord's Prayer
Our Almighty Heavenly Father, our Almighty Heavenly Mother, who art in heaven, hallowed be Thy names. Thy kingdom come, Thy will be done, on Earth as it is in heaven. Give us this day our daily bread, and forgive us our trespasses, as we forgive those who trespass against us. Lead us not into temptation but deliver us from evil. Amen.

The Hail Mary Prayer – Four Hail Mary Prayers
Hail Mary, full of graces, the Lords are with Thee. Blessed art You among women and blessed is the fruit of Your womb, Lord Jesus Christ. Holy Mary, Mother of God, pray for us sinners now and at the hour of our death. Amen

The Glory Be to the Father Prayer
"Glory be to the Almighty Heavenly Father" (with the tip of my right-hand fingers, I touch my forehead) "and to the Almighty Heavenly Mother" (I touched the center of my chest) "and to the Son my Lord Jesus Christ" (I touch my left shoulder) "and

to the Holy Spirit" (I touch my right shoulder) "as it was in the beginning, is now, and ever shall be world without end. Amen."

After I utter each mystery, I meditate by creating scenarios according to each mystery.

For this chapter, I chose the Glorious Mysteries. The Glorious Mysteries are dedicated to Wednesdays and Sundays of each week. I start by holding the crucifix of the rosary with my right-hand fingers, make the sign of the cross, and say: "In the Name of the Almighty Heavenly Father (forehead), and of the Almighty Heavenly Mother (chest), and of the Son my Lord Jesus Christ (left shoulder), and of the Holy Spirit (right shoulder). Amen."

The First Glorious Mystery— The Resurrection of Jesus Christ

I close my eyes. I meditate by quietly recalling the time when my Lord Jesus Christ resurrected from the dead. In my mind, I see Archangel Michael break the rock that covered the tomb where the lifeless body of my Lord Jesus Christ was laid to rest. Archangel Michael stands at the entrance, guarding the tomb. The Almighty Heavenly Father, the Almighty Heavenly Mother, the Holy Spirit, Archangel Gabriel, and Archangel Raphael appear inside the tomb where the lifeless body of our Lord Jesus Christ was laid to rest. I see the Almighty Heavenly Father standing at the left side of the lifeless body of Jesus. I see Archangel Raphael standing at the right side of the Father. Archangel Raphael is comforting the Almighty Heavenly Mother and the Almighty Heavenly Father. Archangel Raphael gently removes the cloth that covered Jesus's face. I see the Holy Spirit standing at the head of Jesus, staring at His lifeless body.

I see the Almighty Heavenly Mother standing at the right side of the lifeless body of Jesus. Archangel Gabriel stands at the left side of the Almighty Heavenly Mother. Archangel Gabriel whispers into the right ear of Jesus and says, "My Lord Jesus Christ, it is time to rise." My Lord Jesus Christ slowly opens His eyes. Our Lord Jesus Christ sees familiar faces, and He smiles.

Archangel Gabriel and Archangel Raphael remove the remaining linen cloth that covers the body of our Lord Jesus Christ. The Almighty Heavenly Father, the Almighty Heavenly Mother, Archangel Raphael, Archangel Gabriel, and the Holy Spirit help my Lord Jesus Christ to a sitting position. Our Lord Jesus Christ gives each of Them a big hug. The Almighty Heavenly Mother receives hugs and kisses from Her beloved Son. They assist our Lord Jesus Christ to stand. Archangel Michael looks at the Lord Jesus Christ and says, "We've got You. We've got Your back." The Almighty Heavenly Mother tells Her Son that it is time to return to heaven. The Lord Jesus Christ lovingly informs His Mother that He has to see His disciples first. He tells His Heavenly Parents to go ahead, and He will follow shortly. The Almighty Heavenly Mother advises Archangel Michael, Archangel Gabriel, and Archangel Raphael to stay behind to protect Her beloved Son. The Holy Spirit volunteers to stay with the three archangels and our Lord Jesus Christ.

The three archangels guard our Lord Jesus Christ when Mary Magdalene meets Him and when He appears to His disciples.

I pause for one minute, and then I offer thanks to the Almighty Heavenly Father, the Almighty Heavenly Mother, the Lord Jesus Christ, the Holy Spirit, Archangel Michael, Archangel Gabriel, and Archangel Raphael.

Before the Lord Jesus Christ appeared to me, I used to pray ten Hail Marys after I uttered each mystery. One night, the Lord Jesus Christ visited me while I was praying the Holy Rosary. He asked me to pray thirteen Hail Mary prayers after each mystery. I asked Him to explain why. He said that each Hail Mary was offered to the Heavenly Father, the Heavenly Mother, the Holy Spirit, Archangel Michael, Archangel Gabriel, Archangel Raphael, Archangel Uriel, Archangel

Haneil, Archangel Selapheil, Archangel Judeil, the Blessed Mother Mary, Saint Joseph, and Himself. Because my Holy Rosary had only ten beads, I asked my Lord Jesus Christ, the Blessed Mother Mary, Archangel Michael, Archangel Gabriel, and Archangel Raphael to remind me to pray thirteen Hail Mary prayers after each mystery. I used three fingers on my left hand to complete the prayers. It was not easy at first. Now, I have gotten used to it.

The Hail Mary Prayer—Thirteen Hail Mary Prayers

Hail Mary, full of grace, the Lords are with Thee. Blessed art You among women and blessed is the fruit of Your womb, Lord Jesus Christ. Holy Mary, Mother of God, pray for us sinners now and at the hour of our death. Amen.

I pray the "Glory Be to the Father" Prayer while making the sign of the cross.

The "Glory Be to the Father" Prayer

"Glory be to the Almighty Heavenly Father" (with the tip of my right-hand fingers, I touch my forehead) "and to the Almighty Heavenly Mother" (I touched the center of my chest) "and to the Son my Lord Jesus Christ" (I touch my left shoulder) "and to the Holy Spirit" (I touch my right shoulder) "as it was in the beginning, is now, and ever shall be world without end. Amen."

The Second Glorious Mystery— The Ascension of the Lord Jesus Christ to Heaven

I close my eyes. I meditate and quietly recall what happened in heaven with our Lord Jesus Christ's imminent return to the Kingdom of His Parents.

In my mind, I picture the Almighty Heavenly Mother and the Almighty Heavenly Father waiting patiently for the return of their beloved Son. The three archangels and the Holy Spirit accompany Jesus to heaven.

As soon as They see their Son enter the kingdom, They run toward Him. They both hug Him and tell Him they missed Him. The Almighty Heavenly Father steps aside and watches His wife cry with tears of joy running down Her cheeks. The Almighty Heavenly Father also cries, along with everyone in the Kingdom. The Heavenly Father, Jesus, and the Heavenly Mother walk toward the throne. The Lord Jesus Christ sits at the right side of His Almighty Heavenly Father and Mother. Everyone rejoices. The guardian angels, cherubs, and seraphim sound the trumpets. Joyous sounds fill His Kingdom. A big celebration happens in heaven.

I pause for about one minute while offering thanks to the Heavenly Father, Mother, Jesus, and the archangels.

I pray the Lord's Prayer, thirteen Hail Marys, and the "Glory Be to the Father" Prayer.

The Third Glorious Mystery—
The Descent of the Holy Ghost Upon the Apostles

I close my eyes and quietly recall how the third mystery unfolded. This is what I picture in my mind. The Holy Ghost descends to the apostles and fills them with wisdom, intelligence, courage, and strength to continue the Lord Jesus Christ's teachings.

I pause for one minute while I offer thank-you prayers. I pray the Lord's Prayer, thirteen Hail Mary prayers, and the "Glory Be to the Father" Prayer.

The Fourth Glorious Mystery—
The Assumption of the Blessed Virgin Mary to Heaven.

My belief is that after our Lord Jesus Christ's ascension to heaven, He visited the Blessed Mother Mary on countless occasions. He comforted His earthly mother. He told the Blessed Mother Mary that His Heavenly Parents were waiting for her arrival in heaven. I believe that our Lord Jesus Christ prepared His earthly mother for her arrival in heaven.

I close my eyes and quietly picture in my mind the moment the Blessed Virgin Mary arrives in heaven. I see the Lord Jesus Christ waiting for her. The three archangels and the Holy Spirit guard the Blessed Mother Mary on her way to heaven. As soon as Jesus sees His earthly mother enter His Kingdom, He runs toward her. He gives her big hugs and kisses her cheeks, forehead, and hands. Tears roll down her cheeks, and Jesus wipes away His own tears. He kisses her on the cheeks and forehead repeatedly. He comforts her and tells her that He loves her. He tells her that from now on, she will live in His Kingdom.

The Blessed Virgin Mary hugs her beloved Son and tells Him how much she missed Him. She kisses her Son's cheeks, forehead, and hands. Lord Jesus Christ takes the Blessed Mother Mary to the Almighty Heavenly Father and the Almighty Heavenly Mother. They hug each other, and the women cry. After a short while, the Lord Jesus Christ shows the Blessed Mother Mary His Kingdom and introduces Her to everyone. He tells His earthly mother that His Parents' Kingdom is also His Kingdom. He says, "I am your Son, and My Kingdom is also your kingdom. From now on, no man can separate the Son of God from His two mothers."

I pause for about one minute while offer thank-you prayers. I say the Lord's Prayer, thirteen Hail Marys, and the "Glory Be to the Father" Prayer.

The Fifth Glorious Mystery— The Coronation of the Blessed Virgin Mary as the Queen of Heaven and Earth

I close my eyes and quietly picture what happened at that very moment in heaven. I see the Lord Jesus Christ speak to His

Lord Jesus Christ appeared to Two Sisters Year 2013 to 2014

Almighty Heavenly Father and Almighty Heavenly Mother prior to the Blessed Mother Mary's arrival in heaven. My belief is that to honor the Blessed Virgin Mary, the Almighty Heavenly Father and the Almighty Heavenly Mother task the Blessed Mother Mary with a position: Queen of Heaven and Earth. The Blessed Virgin Mary accepts her new position. The Almighty Heavenly Father and Mother inform our Lord Jesus Christ and the Blessed Virgin Mary to do everything They can to save humankind. They have full access to all heavenly capabilities that They need to save every single human being on Earth. Lord Jesus Christ and the Blessed Mother Mary nod.

Lord Jesus Christ looks at His earthly mother and tells her that He has plans. He tells her He will not suffer and die on the cross like before. He says, "This time, I will appear to people I choose. I will appear to the chosen people with Archangel Michael, Archangel Gabriel, and Archangel Raphael. The chosen people will know that it is Me. The chosen people will become My messengers. These will be people with kind hearts and minds who listen and obey My messengers. I have done the hardest job on Earth. People who attend church services know what I have done. Many people attend church services but fail to do the hardest jobs of all: to render help to the poorest of the poor, to take care of the sickest of the sick, to provide food for my hungry people, to pick up the spoon and feed the weak one, to fill up a glass with clean water and help the weak one to drink, and to gather materials and build safe homes for the homeless. My people must extend their kindness to the strangers and neighbors. I have shown them My works.

"There are so many rich people on Earth, but they only share their time, success, and wealth to immediate family members and close friends. Lucky are those who donate money to charities. What matters to Me most is for the fortunate people to visit and take care of the poorest of the poor and the sickest of the sick, to provide food and water for the hungry and thirsty people, and to provide safe shelter for those who do not have one. The poor people are My people, too." Lord Jesus Christ looks at the Blessed Mother Mary and tells her They have so much work to do.

I pause for one minute, and then I pray the Lord's Prayer, thirteen Hail Marys, and the "Glory Be to the Father" Prayer. I am not done praying the Holy Rosary yet.

This miracle happened in the fall of 2015. I was inside Saint Joseph Catholic Church. It was a Wednesday, and I was on the fifth Glorious Mystery. While saying the Hail Mary prayer, I felt a strong presence of energies envelope me. I completed praying the ten Hail Mary prayers. I prayed the "Glory Be to the Father" Prayer, and I was about to pray the "Hail, Holy Queen" Prayer when suddenly a strong presence of energy guided my right-hand fingers to the next bead. The strong presence of energy coached me to continue praying the Holy Rosary. I was puzzled because this was not what I was taught. I felt a soothing, cool, airy touch guide my right-hand fingers and move them toward the next bead toward the crucifix. I realized I was heading back to where I started.

I paused and stared at the statue of the Blessed Virgin Mary. Quietly I said, "Okay, Thy will be done." A strong presence of energy was all around me. A soft female voice told me to pray the Lord's Prayer, so I did. Then my fingers moved to the next three beads, and at each bead, I prayed the Hail Mary Prayer. I added one Hail Mary Prayer to dedicate to the Almighty Heavenly Mother. The last bead I prayed was the "Glory Be to the Father" Prayer, and then my fingers moved to the crucifix and prayed the "Hail, Holy Queen" Prayer. The starting point of the Holy Rosary Prayer is the end-point of the Holy Rosary Prayer.

The "Hail, Holy Queen" Prayer
Hail, Holy Queen, Mother of Mercy, hail our life, our sweetness, and our hope. To Thee do we cry, poor banished children of

Eve. To Thee do we send up our sighs, mourning and weeping in this valley of tears. Turn then, most gracious advocate, Thine eyes of mercy toward us. And after this, our exile, show unto us the blessed fruit of Thy womb, Lord Jesus Christ.

O Clement, O Loving, O Sweet Blessed Mother Mary.

Pray for us, O Holy Mother of God, that we will be made worthy in the promises of our Lord Jesus Christ. Amen.

I made the sign of the cross on my body. I remained quiet for a minute.

A stronger presence of cool air hugged me for about ten seconds; it was very soothing and loving. The cool air slowly dissipated. Since then, I have prayed the Holy Rosary like that. I continue to receive so many blessings in my life and share them with people who need help. The feeling of joy, contentment, peacefulness, and calmness inside my heart and mind is beyond compare.

The Other Mysteries of the Holy Rosary

<u>The five Joyful Mysteries are dedicated every Monday and Saturday</u>
1. The Annunciation
2. The Visitation
3. The Birth of our Lord Jesus Christ
4. The Presentation of our Lord Jesus Christ
5. The Finding of our Lord Jesus Christ in the Temple

<u>The five Sorrowful Mysteries are dedicated every Tuesday and Friday</u>
1. The Agony in the Garden
2. The Scourging at the Pillar
3. The Crowning with Thorns
4. The Carrying of the Cross
5. The Crucifixion and Death of our Lord Jesus Christ on the Cross

<u>The five Luminous Mysteries are dedicated every Thursday</u>
1. The Baptismal of our Lord Jesus Christ in the Jordan River
2. The Wedding at Cana
3. The Proclamation of the Kingdom
4. The Transfiguration
5. The Institution of the Eucharist

As I mentioned earlier, I meditate each mystery of the Holy Rosary. I close my eyes and think quietly about each mystery. I construct a story about each one.

The Miracles Inside St. Joseph Catholic Church

It was January 4, 2016, inside Saint Joseph Church. I was praying the Holy Rosary when I smelled roses. The fragrance was light, and it remained in front of me for about five seconds before it disappeared. Then the fragrance came back and remained in front of me for another five seconds before it disappeared again. The fragrance came back for the last time, and this time the fragrance remained for about ten seconds before it disappeared.

On February 5, 2016, inside Saint Joseph Church, I was praying the Holy Rosary, and suddenly I smelled roses again. This time, the fragrance was bold. The fragrance stood in front of me, and then I felt energy hug me. My eyes widened. I stared at the statue of the Blessed Mother Mary and said, "Thank you very much for the miracles." I conversed with her and asked her to be by my side when I take care of patients and troubled families, friends, neighbors, and coworkers. I told her that the Lord Jesus Christ, Archangel Michael, Archangel Gabriel, and Archangel Raphael were by my side also. I asked the Blessed Mother Mary to always guide me to the right path and to protect my son and me from known and unknown enemies. I invited the Blessed Mother Mary to be by my side when I prayed the Holy Rosary whether in my bedroom, at church, or at work.

Lord Jesus Christ appeared to Two Sisters Year 2013 to 2014

I completed praying the Holy Rosary. I got up and lit candles. I smelled the fragrance of roses on my nurse's uniform, my skin, and my hair. I offered short prayers, made the sign of the cross, and exited the church. I was outside the church and noticed that the fragrance of roses was stuck to my nurse's uniform, my jacket, my hair, and my skin. I smiled, looked up and said, "Thank You very much." I drove back to work, and the fragrance slowly disappeared.

When I prayed the Holy Rosary inside my bedroom, inside Saint Joseph Catholic Church, and inside the small chapel of Saint Patrick, cool breezes of air suddenly appeared and touched my face and arms and hugged my entire body. I continue to experience this blessing daily since the end of 2015. It is a comforting feeling.

I am sharing my experiences with you in the hope that it can help and comfort you. I am a sinner, yet miracles continue to happen to me. I learned that it is never too late to repent of my sins. I converse with the Almighty Heavenly Father, the Almighty Heavenly Mother, the Lord Jesus Christ, the Holy Spirit, the Blessed Virgin Mother, and the archangels. They love when we talk to Them. I always tell Them thank You. Remember, we were created according to Their own image and likeness. They love to talk to you, too.

When I talk to my Lord Jesus Christ and the archangels, I recall the way They looked when they appeared to me at the altar of the Holy Infant Jesus of Prague, inside the Chapel of the Traveling Infant Jesus, and at the altar of Our Lady of Fatima. I feel good, protected, blessed, loved, lifted, content, peaceful, and complete. I am happy inside out. It is difficult to describe all my feelings. You, too, can experience this feeling. Different religions have called the Lord Jesus Christ by different names. He is adored and praised by many religions. He is humankind's only Savior. Accept Him with all your heart and mind. Follow His works. His works are pure kindness. Open your heart to the poorest of the poor. The Lord Jesus Christ will appear to you unconditionally. You and I must follow His teachings and hard works. He helped strangers and poor people. You and I can follow His teachings. You and I can give unconditional love to the poor, the sick and dying, the homeless, and the hopeless. Repent all your sins, and return to Him. Never repeat the same sin again. The Lord Jesus Christ and Archangel Michael, Archangel Gabriel, and Archangel Raphael will appear to you.

The Lord Jesus Christ is asking us to have a servant's heart, mind, and hands. The true meaning of unconditional love and kindness is Jesus Christ.

Conclusion

I always believe in my Lord Jesus Christ. I surrendered my life to Him. He saved me from the hands of the enemies. He saved me from rocket and mortar attacks. When He appeared to me, I thanked Him for saving me, my airmen, soldiers, sailors, marines, and the Wounded Warriors. It was not difficult for me to take care of the wounded enemies at all because at the end of the day, the wounded enemies were doing exactly what they were told to do. I promised myself that one day I would visit my family in Davao City and visit the miraculous statue of the Traveling Infant Jesus Christ.

I looked for the statue of the Traveling Infant Jesus Christ, but I could not find it. No one knew where it was. My Lord Jesus Christ felt my devastation and heartache. Quietly, He led me to the location. The Lord Jesus Christ appeared to my sister and me. He has dark brown skin. I believe that His earthly mother, the Blessed Mother Mary, has brown skin as well. The Blessed Mother Mary and Lord Jesus Christ are my Holy Grail. The Archangel Michael, Archangel Gabriel, and Archangel Raphael appeared to me when Jesus Christ appeared to me inside the Chapel of the Traveling Infant Jesus. They blessed me. I am sharing with you these blessings hoping they inspire you.

I am a sinner just like you. I have violated speed limits and gotten caught. I was upset that I got caught, but I paid the speeding tickets. I told white lies to my siblings so I wouldn't offend their feelings. I apologized quietly and asked forgiveness from my Lord Jesus Christ. It is a bit challenging being the oldest of the five siblings. I get angry when drivers fail to use their signals before changing lanes or when telemarketers call my home phone when I am praying the Holy Rosary. I ask for forgiveness. I repented all my sins and asked our Lord Jesus Christ to help me not to sin anymore. I prayed to the Almighty Heavenly Mother and the Blessed Mother Mary to guide me in taking care of my only child. I love my son very much.

I attend Catholic church services whenever I can. I continue to visit Saint Joseph Church and Saint Patrick Chapel during my lunch breaks and pray the Holy Rosary. I pray to the Holy Rosary on a daily basis. I extend my kindness to friends, family, patients, and strangers. Upon arriving at work, I close my door, and I pray inside my screening room. I pray for every nurse, provider, administrative employee, and patient, as well as myself. I pray that the Divine Family will grant all of us a wonderful, happy, safe day at work.

I placed the statue of the Holy Infant Jesus of Prague across from my bed so that I can see Him and talk to Him while I am lying down. I believe that there are four processes in becoming a Jesus Christ follower. The four processes must be present to become His true follower: 1) listen to and learn from His words, 2) follow His works and examples, 3) love one another unconditionally, and 4) render kindness to unfortunate people and strangers.

Listen to the Almighty Heavenly Father and the Lord Jesus Christ's words by reading the Holy Bible and following all His works—the miracles He performed before He was crucified and died on the cross. Many of us attend Sunday church services; others attend church services every day. We have learned so much from the church services, but what I have noticed is that the majority of the people who attend church services leave what they learned inside the church. Once they leave the church, they change. I noticed that many of them are selfish, cruel, mean, jealous, and harmful to their coworkers, neighbors, and families. Coworkers make up untrue stories to harm and hurt a person. It happened to me. I offered them all to my Lord Jesus Christ. If anyone harms me or hurts me, they harm and hurt my Lord Jesus Christ. Do not throw away what you learned from church services or ignore what you learned from the Holy Scriptures; apply them all. Think of works that our Lord Jesus did before He was crucified and died on the cross. He was compassionate, very kind, and patient, and above all, he loved all of us unconditionally. Lord Jesus Christ rendered kindness and unconditional love to all men and women. He gave His life to save all races. He did not discriminate. Let us follow in His footsteps.

People who are blessed with wealth and knowledge must visit poor neighborhoods and see for themselves what the less unfortunate people need to live each day. Bring a loaf of bread, a pound of rice or corn, canned goods, sugar, and coffee. Bring clean used clothes, blankets, and towels. Check the condition of their homes. A surgeon can donate his time going to poor cities and rendering his specialties to the less unfortunate people. Nurses can volunteer their time in any community delivering hot meals to the unfortunate people and senior citizens and providing vaccinations and health screenings.

Ask for help by praying to the Almighty Heavenly Father, Almighty Heavenly Mother, our Lord Jesus Christ, the Blessed Mother Mary, the Holy Spirit, Archangel Michael, Archangel Gabriel, Archangel Raphael, Archangel Uriel, Archangel Haniel, Archangel Selapheil, and Archangel Judeil. Pray the Holy Rosary. Have a servant's heart, mind, and hands.

The Lord Jesus Christ appeared to me unconditionally. I am His messenger. I wrote this book because He asked me to. English is not my first language, and I am not a writer. It was a difficult task, but I made it through. My secret is this: Before I start writing, I call my Lord Jesus Christ, Archangel Gabriel, Archangel Uriel, and the Holy Spirit. I talk to Them. I ask Them to bless me with good health, plenty of energy, and the ability to find the right words.

Lord Jesus Christ loves you so much that He is doing everything He can to save you. Jesus loves humans very much. He appeared to me wearing a faded green chambray shirt and faded brown cropped pants as warning colors. What if the faded green and faded brown colors meant that the time of humans' existence on planet Earth is getting shorter? What if the faded green and faded brown colors mean that human existence is coming to an end soon? Lord Jesus Christ has given us warnings, and we must listen. He is like our loving parents, always giving us warnings. If you do good things, you get rewarded. If you do bad things and get caught, you get punished.

Humans are destructive beings. Everything that the Divine Family has given to us we either harmed or destroyed totally. Humans have destroyed the forests; we caused global warming. We caused the soil/land to erode. Humans use harmful chemicals to protect their plants, and in return the harmful chemicals are absorbed by the soil and poison the soil, lakes, rivers, and oceans. We must unite and save each other and save Earth.

I am sharing with you the way I pray the Holy Rosary, my beliefs, and my experiences. It does not matter who you are and what sins you have committed in your life. I am a sinner myself. The Lord Jesus Christ has asked you to repent and return to Him. It is never too late to repent of all the sins you have committed and return to our Lord Jesus Christ. Only through Him can you and I enter the Kingdom of His Heavenly Father and Heavenly Mother. It is only through Him that you and I can be saved.

Kindness is a universal law, and it starts with you.

www.ingramcontent.com/pod-product-compliance
Lightning Source LLC
Chambersburg PA
CBHW050043080526
44586CB00014B/1428